Strength

AND

Dignity

Dear Christine,
    Thank you for all of
your love + support!
    Lots of Love~
        Shelly Rivelli

Shelley Rivelli

ISBN 978-1-64349-557-6 (paperback)
ISBN 978-1-64349-558-3 (digital)

Christian Faith Publishing, Inc.
832 Park Avenue
Meadville, PA 16335
www.christianfaithpublishing.com

Printed in the United States of America

To my mother. A true woman of strength and dignity. Thank you for always being my biggest fan and for encouraging me by saying that everything I write is "your favorite one." I love you.

Contents

Preface

Strength and Dignity

"She is clothed with strength and dignity, and she
laughs without fear of the future" (Proverbs 31:25).

Who is this woman?
   She is a woman who trusts in the Lord. A woman who
has bonded her heart to Jesus. A woman who has come to understand her worth in Christ. Her strength is in Jesus, and her dignity is
in his love story for her.

The beauty of this strength and dignity is that it is available for
all believers. Too often, we reserve dignity for those who appear to
have their lives all together. We consider others to be dignified by
their outward appearances (where they live, what they drive, what
they wear). The truth is, a woman clothed in dignity simply knows
the love of her Savior and in return loves others with his love. A
woman clothed in strength and dignity does not allow her situation
in life to define her. She finds herself in the midst of hardships, poverty, and strife, and lives her life out based on who she is in Christ.
She trusts the Lord for all of her needs, therefore, can hold her head
high and walk with a confidence and lightness that only comes from
a relationship with Jesus. She walks life out with Christ, believing he
will help her to be whom she was created to be.

Empowering others in Christ is a high priority for this woman.
She desires to see others live in victory. Her heart breaks for the least
of these because she sees herself in their lives . . . in their eyes. She
understands that they feel worthless and less because they are poor.

Because they don't have what the world says that they should. They feel like they are less important because of where they live and the messy stories of their lives.

Who is this woman? She is me. I am the woman at the well. I am the woman who reached out to touch the hem of Jesus. I am the woman he saved from being stoned. I am the woman clothed in strength in dignity.

My guess is you find yourself in the lives and hearts of these women as well. I am writing this book for you. I am writing this book for me. May the words in these pages lead us closer to Jesus.

The Garden

As I walk across my backyard, dragging the hose to water my garden, I can almost hear the land below me crying out in thirst. It is begging to be watered, rained on, nurtured, and replenished. My bare feet are being stabbed by the hay that used to be grass. I approach the garden and look around at the yard that used to feed my soul with its beauty. It is dying. Dying in stages that I can relate to, that I easily recognize. It is dying in stages that reflect different times in my own life and possibly yours as well.

The area of the yard that is most painful to look at . . . that takes my breath away . . . is where there is no longer life. I try to soak it with water from the hose, and it will not receive it. I cry. It fills me with a familiar ache as the words *hopeless, worthless, unloved,* and *useless* come to mind. This has been me. I have felt this way. What causes us to feel this way? Failed relationships, abandonment, rejection, death of a loved one . . . disappointment. There are times when we feel this way, and we don't know why. We just do. Unfortunately, it is during this time that I find it the most difficult to receive the words and encouragement from others. It is during this time that I know that the words from my heavenly Father could save me, but I battle with reading his words or allowing others to speak them to me. My prayers are through gritted teeth, and my heart is hard.

The grass that has withered to brittle hay surrounds me. I hear the words *angry, prickly, broken,* and *weary.* I am irritable and easily offended. I have more life in me than during barren times, but I use that life to fight. Not fight for peace or joy . . . just to fight. I am ugly on the inside. I am the worst version of myself. Thank God for his grace and mercy. Thank God, he lives in so many people who have become the fabric of my life. I claw my way out through that Grace, through his softening touch to my heart. I am fed, replenished, and watered by just the right scriptures, sermons, songs. I am brought back to life by his touch alone. That touch often comes through an act of kindness by someone who has been there, who listens, who understands, who recognizes the hay.

The areas that have not been as burnt by the sun (the circumstances of life) remain green. Barely. I am here often. I am holding on. I am doing my devotionals, trying to attend Bible studies, doing my best to attend church, and paying attention to the words and not the chaos in my mind. I am doing well . . . That's what my answer is to those who ask. I'm hanging on.

I continue to walk across my yard. I am discouraged at the revelation that has taken place. I approach my garden. I feel a quickening in my Spirit. My garden has been well nourished, watered, and loved. It is flourishing. I am reminded of the times I, too, have been here. I am here when I am trusting the Lord, allowing his words to feed my soul and nourish my Spirit. I am healed and gratefully walking in that healing. I spend time in my Savior's presence. I am still. I am forgiven. I look closely at my garden, and it is producing fruit . . . and because the Lord is faithful, so do I.

John 4:13–14

The Mattress

During my second divorce, I was homeless. My children and I lived with friends and family, as the fabric of my life was falling apart. I woke up every morning, got my children to school, and went to work. I would touch the side of the front door as I walk into the building. The cold brick wall would hold my problems so that I could give my students and coworkers my best. At the end of the day, I would retrieve my problems and carry on until I could put my head on the pillow at night.

My faith at this time was shaky at best. Cliffs Notes version of my first divorce . . . my youthful ignorance and selfish nature were to blame. This time, I was in it for better or worse. I was so afraid of disappointing the Lord (again) that I stayed in a very unhealthy situation for far too long. Being divorced once was bad, and I was pretty sure that twice was the mortal sin. I was so confused. I was honoring God by forgiving and staying. Why wasn't he healing my marriage? Despite my prayers, it became apparent that my marriage was not going to be healed, and I divorced a second time. Not sure that God considered me his daughter any longer, I tried to pick up the pieces of my shattered life and moved my family back home.

Joyless and going through the motions described the next season of my life. I was broke . . . financially and spiritually.

It was during this time that a friend spoke to me about gratitude being a way to rediscover my joy. I was ready to try. I began to thank God for all things in my life. From morning snuggles with my three-year-old to the way the sun made the water look like it was dancing. Every night when I got into bed (seven years later, I still do this), I thanked God for my bed and the warmth of my blankets. One night, I must have been feeling bold, I thanked God for those things but brought to his attention that the mattress had a lot to be desired. Who am I? Divorced twice, and I am bringing up my lumpy mattress to the King of kings? Honestly, I still laugh when I think of this. Thankfully, his name is Mercy.

Fast-forward to Tom. I began spending time with a man from church. Weeks into our friendship, he awkwardly and with hesitation tells me that God has placed on his heart to buy me . . . you guessed it . . . *a mattress*! I had never spoken about my old hand-me-down mattress to anyone. You see, I know scripture. I know that God forgives a contrite heart, and mine surely was. I know that God is close to the brokenhearted, and I know that nothing (even two divorces) can separate me from the love of God. However, those truths were not healing me. So my heavenly Father bought his undeserving daughter a mattress. And my heart began to heal.

Jesus is alive and wants a relationship with us. The words in the Bible are lifesaving and will transform us with God's truth. But time and time again, when those words fall short on my heart, Jesus shows up closer than any dear friend and with the power of a Savior to show me the love of a Father.

PS: I must have watched too many Disney fairy-tale movies when I was a little girl. I am married again . . . to Tom.

The Present

A million years ago, before I had children, I attended a women's conference at my church. I was twenty years old. During the conference, there were breakaway sessions. Pretty confident that the session titled "The Present" would involve parting gifts, I chose to sit in on that one. In the center of each table, there was a beautifully wrapped gift. *Bingo!* However, much to my dismay, the gift was actually a visual representation of the message that was being spoken that day.

The speaker, a mom, spoke about how our words could be gifts of love and encouragement for our children. When she confessed about the times that she had spoken harshly to her children, I judged. When she gave actual examples of what she had said to her children, I judged and thought, *I* would never*!* She encouraged her listeners to wrap a box in beautiful paper and ribbon and place it somewhere in our home as a reminder of what kind words and encouragement could do for our children. How we could be a gift to them. How our words could help heal them. I held back laughter. You need a visual reminder to be kind to your children? What? Twenty-year-old Shelley was a clueless idiot. I kind of want to punch her in the face. Parenting is harder than I ever imagined it would be. It has brought me to my knees more times than I can count. I should have listened closer that day for sure.

I am a special education teacher and a behavior analyst. Part of my job is parent training, and I am so blessed to work with the most amazing parents. I swear I learn from them as much they learn from me. It is incredibly important to me that the parents I work with

13

know that they can share with me in a judgment-free zone. I often share stories about my children and ways that I handled situations and ways I could have done better. There are times, regardless of my degrees and training, I just get it wrong.

Parenting children is difficult . . . every single day. Raising children with special needs brings its own set of challenges. I have a twenty-year-old daughter with anxiety and depression and a thirteen-year-old son diagnosed with obsessive compulsive disorder. You would think that being educated about their struggles would elicit compassion and patience. Not always. I have yelled at my daughter and told her that she would "feel better" if she was "more grateful," and when my son has taken thirty minutes to walk in the back door, I have walked out the front. I have yelled at him to "just" get dressed, wash his hair, stop washing his hands, knock it off—"stop being irrational."

What about those mornings when you have lost your mind all the way to school, and after you dropped them off, you wanted to run into the school, find them, hug them, and beg them for forgiveness? I have locked myself in my bathroom, faked sick to stay in bed, called friends to talk me off of a ledge, taken pictures of toothpaste in the sink as evidence, and made up excuses to go to Wal-Mart and then drove around in my car weeping.

Parenting is hard.

To all the parents reading this, if you have said the unimaginable to your children and still feel guilty because of it, let it go. Your love and kindness outweighs anything you have said. You were scared, weary, disappointed, angry . . . battle worn. I get it. I am constantly asking God for wisdom because I know this to be true . . . He handpicked me to be Haley's, Christopher's, and Benjamin's mom. Guess what? He handpicked you to be the mom of your children as well. Just you. God knows our children, and he has equipped us to have the right words to meet their inner most needs. I have learned to ask him to help me be the mom he created me to be. I have found scriptures that I want my children to live in and speak them over their lives and minds.

"You are fearfully and wonderfully made" (Psalm 139:14), "You have the mind of Christ" (1 Corinthians 2:16), "God has not given you a spirit of fear; but of power and love, and sound mind" (2 Timothy 1:7), "You will honor your mother . . ." (Matthew 19:19). Just kidding, but that's a good one.

Don't try to parent alone. It's just too messy. Turn to the Lord for guidance and strength. He will equip you for the most difficult job on earth and give you rest when you need it and restore your mind, when you've lost it.

Salvation

There is a coffee place in town that I go to once in a while. Okay . . . every single day for the last thirteen years. I walked in recently and overheard a conversation between a customer and two employees. The customer was telling the employees that being a Christian and going to heaven really just comes down to being "a good person." I sat quietly as she spoke and waited patiently for her to leave. As soon as the door closed behind her, I leaned against the counter and very firmly said, "Don't believe her!" When the employees, whom I love as family, reenact this, they pretend to leap over the counter and scream. It's a crack-up, and I may have indeed looked that passionate . . . AKA crazy.

It sounds like good news . . . you just have to be a good person, when actually it is the worst news ever. Can you imagine? Your behavior determines where you spend eternity. I would be in trouble, for sure! We all would.

So here's the truth . . . the real *good news*! (Brought to you through The Roman Road.) Truly the best gift we could be given. Thankfully, we cannot earn it, buy it, or be good enough to receive it.

1. God is perfect and *holy*. For *all* have sinned and fall short of the glory of God (Romans 3:23).
2. But God demonstrates his own love toward us in a way that while we were still sinners, Christ died for us (Romans 5:8).
3. For the wages of sin is death (hell, people), but the gift of God is eternal life in Jesus our Lord (Romans 6:23). Jesus died in our place.

4. For with the heart, one believes unto righteousness, and with the mouth, confession is made unto salvation. For the scripture says, "Whoever believes in him will not be put to shame" (Romans 10:10–11).
5. For "whoever calls on the name of the Lord shall be saved" (Romans 10:13).

Salvation is a personal relationship with Jesus. It is believing that he died on the cross for the forgiveness of your sins. He is knocking on the door of your heart. Jesus will not force himself on you, but he is there with the invitation of a lifetime. He invites you to ask him into your life. He invites you to receive the gift of eternal life. He invites you into a personal relationship where he is Lord over your life, your Savior, your peace, your best friend. You will never be the same.

I have shared this with people who feel that they have lived a life so terrible that, somehow, they are disqualified for this gift. Here is the truth *anyone* and *everyone* who trusts in him will not be put to shame. Jesus came and died for everyone. You can't be good enough to earn this gift. Jesus took your sins to the cross with him. Once you confess your sins and ask Jesus into your heart and life, your sins are wiped away, and you are made clean. Now that's *good news*!

If you want to ask Jesus to come into your life, forgive your sins, and begin your new life getting to know who Jesus is, and have a relationship with him, you can say this prayer.

"Heavenly Father, thank you for loving me. Lord Jesus, thank you for dying for me. I confess that I am a sinner. I repent of my sins. Please forgive me. Jesus, please come into my life. Thank you for my salvation. Amen."

And now the angels in heaven celebrate. I am celebrating. In this life that can be so dark, Jesus will be your light and joy.

Please feel free to contact me with questions or to simply celebrate with you. The book of John is a great place to start in this new journey. I love you, and I am so proud of you.

I want to thank Pastor Bob Howard for inspiring me to write this as many of these words are his words. Thank you for being a faithful man of God and a shepherd to so many.

Tacoma

No longer able to afford living in New York as a single mother, I moved my family to my home town in Massachusetts. My daughter, Haley, struggled with this transition. She was away from her father, her family, and her friends. Making new friends did not come easily, and Haley was discouraged and lonely. It was during this dark time that Haley's heavenly Father shined his amazing love and light into her life. God chose to do this in a way that only he knew would speak directly to her heart and change her life. He did this through a horse named Tacoma. Haley was eleven. Her girlfriend introduced Haley to a barn and this horse. I've never seen my daughter so willing and ambitious to wake up before the sun and head off to her new favorite place to be with her very large and beautiful best friend. Just a little girl, regardless of the weather, Haley would muck stalls and work as hard as she could. She would be paid in the opportunity to ride Tacoma.

Two years passed, and we received notification that Tacoma was being sold. I was doing my best to make ends meet. Buying Tacoma and caring for him was not in the cards for us, and Tacoma left the barn. I would have done just about anything to stop this from happening, but there just wasn't a way. Haley suffered a sadness that stayed with her. She kept pictures close by and memories in her heart. We eventually looked at other horses, but nothing ever fit. Haley took riding lessons, but she missed Tacoma gravely. A couple of years ago, she asked me if she could put an ad in the paper to look for him. We chose not to.

Fall 2015, Haley left for her freshman year in college, another transition that did not go well for my daughter. We spoke a lot during this time about her heavenly Father's unfailing love for her. I continued to do my best to pour what truths I knew into Haley's life . . . promising her that God had a plan for her. I tried to encourage her that we never know what may be coming right around the corner. Meanwhile, I was praying a mama's urgent prayer that God would once again speak to Haley's heart the way only her heavenly Father could.

In November, I came home and walked into my kitchen to find my precious daughter sobbing. When I say sobbing, I mean ugly, shoulders shaking, unintelligible crying. When I asked her to please tell me what was wrong, she whispered, "He found him." I knew. God answered my prayers for a little girl who was giving up.

Seven years had passed. In a sequence of events that only God could orchestrate Tacoma was 30 minutes away. Remember the girl-friend that introduced her to Tacoma? This girl's friend's grandfather had recently purchased Tacoma. One day the two girls were together sharing pictures and Haley's childhood friend said, "Hey, I know that horse." She then proceeded to call Haley and this is where I enter the kitchen. (Did you follow all of that? Well Done!) Isn't God incredible? It gets better . . . hold on. I secretly contact Haley's childhood friend asking if I could be bold enough to request a visit with Tacoma. Just to provide Haley with some closure. She arranges a visit. I tell Haley I have a surprise for her. The surprise didn't last long. As soon as we enter the town where Tacoma is living she starts to cry. She knows. We arrive to the barn and meet the granddaughter; you know the one sharing the pictures. She explains to us that her grandfather is on the phone with a potential buyer and will be right down to meet us. "Buyer?" I ask. "Yes," She says. "He is selling Tacoma." I'm not sure who said the next statement but it appeared to come out of my mouth. "I will buy him!" Well the rest is history. I had no idea what the grandfather was asking for him or where Tacoma would live. What I did know . . . He was Haley's.

I drove home that day with praise on my lips and confidence that God had all the details worked out. He certainly did. We are so blessed. Tacoma couldn't be in a better place. He is boarded at a fabulous barn and they love him like one of their very own. He is so happy and well cared for. God knew this was the place for him as I'm sure he touched the owner's heart to take in a new addition to the herd right before the winter months. We are so thankful!

Haley will tell you this is her story of God's love. I will tell you that God saved a little girl with this horse, and I love what Tacoma represents. He is tangible evidence that God sees our hurt, that he never forgets, and that he will redeem that sadness. I am always saying, "God has a plan." We often can't see a way or understand why things happen. I am learning to trust, no matter what, because you never know what is right around the corner, and when it is from our heavenly Father's heart directly to ours, it is beyond what we could imagine!

Psalm 13:5–6
Psalm 33:22
Matthew 6:33

Happy Father's Day

Wanting God to know me and being years away from knowing the truth of Psalm 139, I wrote a letter to him to introduce myself. I was six. I told him my name and all about the important details of my six-year-old life. I left the letter and my school picture (for identification purposes) on the altar of the Trinity Episcopal Church. Because that it where God lived.

As I grew older, my theology improved. I knew I could speak to my heavenly Father, but how I loved to write him letters. When I felt badly about my behavior, I wrote God a letter. When I wanted my period (all the other girls had it, and I was sure my boobs would finally come), I wrote God a letter. When I wanted a boy to like me, I wrote a God a letter. When I was hurt, I wrote God a letter. When my family was in need, I wrote God a letter.

As an adult, I continue to write to God. I want to share with you my Father's Day letter to my heavenly Father.

Dear heavenly Father,

Thank you for being there when I took my first step, graduated from Humpty Dumpty Nursery School, lost my first tooth, learned to ride my bike, and for that watch I wanted, with all of my heart, for my birthday.

Thank you for sending me to Hickory Hill Summer Camp and for my childhood days at the beach . . . well, except for the summer I got the chicken pox. Although, I am thankful for the coloring book and brand-new crayons. Thank you for being there when I got my license, graduated high school, and got into The University of New Hampshire.

Thank you for your protection and for saving my life when I was rebellious and stupid. Thank you for always correcting me in love when I deserved to be brought behind the woodshed. Thank you for always forgiving me. When I have been the worst version of myself, thank you for always showing me a better way.

Thank you for my 1986 Ford Escort wagon, for dear friends, and laughter. Thank you for putting me through college and graduate school. Thank you for the job of my dreams.

When man has cheated and been cruel, thank you for always being faithful and kind. Thank you for not letting me date "you-know-who" and for always having strong open arms when my heart was broken.

Thank you for walking me down the aisle. Thank you for wiping my tears and restoring my faith. Thank you for paying my debt, providing for my children and blessing me beyond measure. You have sealed *grace* on my heart and given me the desires of my heart like only a Father can.

You alone command my destiny. Thank you for my freedom.

You are the Great I Am commanding the stars into the sky, and yet you whisper, "You can do it!" in my ear. You have always been my greatest cheerleader.

Happy Father's Day, Abba Father

Love,
Your beloved

Put Me in, Coach

As God searches all the earth and looks for that very person he is going to ask to be his hands and feet, his eyes fall upon me. He asks, "Whom shall I send?" I stand up tall, boldly shoot my hand into the sky, and shout, "Me, Lord, send me!" The King of all kings pats my head and whispers, "My beloved, I see your heart, but you are just too much work. You are selfish, you complain, you are constantly in need of redirection, and you doubt everything." He continues on with his search.

I recently went to see the movie *Hacksaw Ridge*. I am not going to spoil the movie, but what I will tell you is this . . . Desmond Doss gives new meaning to standing on your convictions and trusting in the Lord. Desmond's walk with the Lord gives amazing insight and revelation to the truth that the same power that raised Jesus from the dead lives in his followers. That power lives in you and in me! What if we each lived in that truth and believed the very thing we are facing today could be conquered by that power. We could be the wife, husband, daughter, son, mother, father, sister, brother, friend, employee, and witness the Lord has asked us to be. What if we studied God's plan for how we should live these roles out and, with his strength, lived them out according to his word? I believe that we would change our households and speak God's love into the lives of those around us. I'm weary of Christians giving lip service to what the Bible says without applying it to their own lives. Especially me, I'm sick of me! I am starting a new chapter . . . one that takes the knowledge I have gained since I was a young girl and actually applying it to my life. I am bringing the gantlet down and screaming, "Enough!" Okay, deep breaths . . .

Here's the good news. This is what the Bible actually says in 2 Chronicles 16:9, "For the eyes of the Lord range throughout the earth to strengthen those whose hearts are fully committed to him." I don't have to do this alone or in my own strength? Can I get an *amen*? The Lord has equipped me with all I will need to live under his word. I will love him with all my heart and soul and mind and love others because I will rely on his love to see me through. I will forgive others because the Lord will remind me of his forgiveness of my sins. I will not judge because I have planks in my own eye. I will stop putting my needs and my feelings first because my Lord led by example in the greatest way possible . . . at the cross.

Let me be upfront and honest . . . I want to live a life worthy of God's calling, but will I do so perfectly and gracefully? Not at all. However, I did mention in the beginning that I am a lot of work. Thank God, he knows my heart.

Romans 8:11

Big Chill Retro Refrigerator

"Seek first his kingdom and his righteousness, and all these things will be given to you as well" (Matthew 6:33).

I have spent most of my life believing "all these things" meant "all the desires" of my heart—that somehow if I was a good enough Christian, I could earn the desires of my heart. The undoing of this belief has been—how do I say this?—confusing and painful.

I want a beach blue Big Chill retro refrigerator. And not in my house in heaven. I want it now, in the land of the living, on Hill Street. I do. I have for quite some time. I have researched it, dreamt about how amazing it will look in my kitchen, and tried to bribe my husband, "But, hun, what if I forgo Christmas and birthday presents for a decade?"

Here's the thing, I also want there to be an end to human trafficking, hate, poverty, and injustice. This is where it gets tricky. I love Jesus, study how he lived, want desperately to share him with others, help people to be set free by knowing him and his love, and I want a $4,000 refrigerator. I may actually think about all of those things equally. Lord, help me. Not joking, in church this morning, the pastor was speaking about the reality of human trafficking, and one second, I was thinking about how I could get involved, and the next, I was wondering if maybe I liked the orange refrigerator better. Stand behind me, Satan.

I am currently facilitating a class that focuses on the book *Falling Free*, by Shannan Martin. On the first day of class, I told the group that although I had read the book months before and more than once, I was along for the ride with them and that I didn't have the answers. Sorry, gang. We have been unpacking the book, as well as scripture, to dig deeper into how Jesus lived and how he calls us to live. It is challenging, and frankly, if I wasn't the "teacher," I would probably bail. Kidding . . . kind of. With topics about living with less, holding on loosely to our time, plans and money, surrendering to God's will always, and loving our neighbors as ourselves, we have had some real and honest conversations. I am growing. I am asking God to align my heart with his and to break my heart for what breaks his and then to walk out in faith. I am praying for the opportunity and courage to share his love and truth with others. I am learning that there is quite a difference between want and need, and I believe that he meets all of my needs and often does give me the desires of my heart. So often.

Over the summer, my daughter, Haley, asked me, "What does Jesus think of money?" I was so moved by the sincerity of the question and also ashamed that I really didn't know the answer. I said, "I believe that Jesus feels that if you have two shirts and someone needs one, you give him one . . . the nicer one." Now I am beginning to believe that if you only have one shirt, you give that away, fully believing that the Lord will provide you with a different shirt. Jesus teaches us how he wants us to love others. There are amazing lessons in Matthew 25 as well as the greatest commandment in Matthew 22:36–40. Actually, just read the entire New Testament. I have always believed that when you see a person in need, you help. Now I am beginning to see that as a Christian, I should be looking for the need. It's not enough to answer the call. I need to be fighting for those that can't and looking for where I can be the hands and feet of Jesus. I need to hold on so loosely to my own plans that I am at the ready to follow the Lord's plans whenever he calls. His plans are always so much better. I will be the first to tell you that a year ago, I told God, "Your will, not my own."

Since then my life has been fun, rewarding, and blessed. I was scared when I said it then and only a bit less scared now. However, imagine if we all lived this way. What world problems could be changed? If I have enough money to buy a fabulous refrigerator, even though mine is perfectly fine, then I have enough money to give away to a cause that will bring freedom to others. Our lives our not our own, dear Christian friends. They never were. They were bought with a price. Let's live out our lives for the One who paid the price. I am right there with you, trying to figure it all out. I want answers and will be asking the Lord to teach me through his word. Let this journey begin.

Not Alone

Faith is the assurance of things hoped for, the conviction of things not seen.

I want you to know I hear you. I hear your questions, and I understand your doubts. I am you. When I hear that someone doesn't believe, has turned away from God, or they have anger toward him, I secretly relate. Faith can be a place of joy and goodness. It can be answered prayer. But what about when it is not? What if what you have prayed for does not come to pass? The child does not get well, the pregnancy doesn't happen, the loved one does not get saved, the loved one dies, he/she isn't set free from addiction, the marriage isn't healed, you are not healed. What if your mountain just won't move? I love the Bible and believe that it is the very words and promises of God. I can do a Bible study on healing and find thirty scriptures that speak of God's promise to heal. But what about when he doesn't? I can find scripture on his promise to protect, comfort, and defend. But what about when he doesn't?

Let me be brutally honest with you. I am not always a good daughter, and I have given *grace* new meaning. Thank you, Lord, for your patience, and I'm hoping you have earplugs when my tantrumming begins. True story. I was recently sitting in a parking lot on the phone with my mother. I was distraught because my daughter has not been freed from her depression, my son's OCD is at an all-time high, and I am having some personal challenges that I can't see getting better. Often, I just surrender and remind myself of the scripture "Trust in the Lord with all of your heart and lean not on your own understanding" (Proverbs 3:5). I want my testimony to be that I trust

the Lord no matter what. I want unmovable faith. I want to understand and accept that I may not have answers this side of heaven but
that I stand on the Word of God and that I know God is good. Guess
what? Not that morning. I was screaming. I can't imagine what the
people going into the coffee place were thinking. I was screaming
that I wanted my testimony to be that I had faith, asked for the healing of my children, and that they were healed. I was yelling, "How
about that gets to be my testimony?" There may have been some
swearing. Sorry, God. Sorry, Mom. So here I am to tell you . . . don't
give up! Please. I know you're weary. I know you doubt. I know you
want to throw in the towel. I don't have answers. But I can tell you
this . . . Jesus does. I know him. He is far too faithful for the likes of
me, but he is anyway. He knows what it feels like to be rejected, to be
forsaken. I can tell you time and time again how he has saved my life.
Although I am no Job, I do know that after my tantrumming is over
and I have asked God for forgiveness, I do stand on his word. Every
time. Sometimes it takes me longer than other times, but I know that
Jesus is my Savior. Not just my Savior that secures my eternity but
the one who saves me daily . . . sometimes from myself. I can look
back and see clearly that some of the most difficult and seemingly
forsaken times were amazing blessings and that he was always right
there with me. God always knows better. Trust him. It is not easy,
and there were times that I was so desperate and so confused that I
couldn't pray. I would just simply whisper, "I trust you. I trust you.
I trust you . . . ." You can do it! Jesus understands your disbelief. Ask
him to help your disbelief. Jesus sees your pain, you are not alone,
and you are loved with an unending love.

Deuteronomy 31:6 and 8.

Growing Up Poor

G rowing up, my family was poor. I guess there are other ways to say it: "humble beginnings" or "low-middle class. But let's be real. We were poor. My father was the breadwinner as well as an alcoholic and gambler. My mother, in addition to raising five children, worked outside of the house as often as she could.

When I was a teenager, I was crazy about this guy. Lying down on the bulkhead cover at my families' apartment, looking up at the stars, he told me that I couldn't be his girlfriend anymore, because my family was poor and his family had money. His parents, Christian parents that I admired, had been encouraging him to stop seeing me for that reason. That breakup confirmed all my fears. I was less. Less valuable, less worthy, less important. This became my inner voice and lens in which I saw myself for decades. Is there something in your life that makes you feel less?

Believing that I am precious to my heavenly Father, I am no longer chained to the shame of my childhood. My value is in Christ's love and his love alone. *As is yours!* Your value isn't defined by the world's opinion or your sin. Jesus overcame the world and defeated sin at the cross.

Set free, I am now able to see my childhood in a different light. My siblings and I are very close. There are a lot of things that bond us together, and I am convinced that one of those things is our ability to laugh about the times that once hurt. One of our favorite stories is how we didn't own a hairdryer but someone had given us a shop vac. We would switch the air to come out of the machine, and we would dry our hair with it. Let us not forget the foam pieces that served as our mattresses and cars that were missing floor pieces and didn't drive in reverse. My brother Doug is a very funny and talented comedian. Our childhood provides a lot of material for him. Laughter can scare away demons. At one of his shows, I was brought to tears of laughter remembering that our milk came out of the cabinet (powdered milk must have been cheaper) and that fried dough was not a special treat for dinner but my mom's way of hiding that it was all we had in the house. My mother had a way of making things fun. Saturday nights were family sleepovers in the living room, and she always made Christmas memorable. One Christmas Eve, during the cabbage patch craze, my mom made our pajamas to wear to bed. In the morning, she had five cabbage patch kids (which she made) sitting on the couch in matching pajamas. I have treasured this memory for thirty-five years. (I am not sure if my children remember what they got last year for Christmas.) The love my mom poured into her children was immeasurable. I didn't know that we teetered on homelessness or that it wasn't normal to wear winter hats to bed in the winter.

What I did know is that the church provided most of our needs, from food to cars. I knew what it felt like to be told no. I knew what wearing hand-me-downs felt like and that my life felt very different from my friend's lives. Anyone who knows me knows how grateful I am for the life I am blessed with. I teach in the town I grew up in and live on a street that I could have only dreamt about as a child. I have more than I should. It is very important for me that my children know about my childhood. My children need to know that their overpriced sneakers no more define who they are than the hand-me-downs of my childhood defined who I was. However, they don't need to know that fried dough for dinner isn't a delicacy. Because it is.

Matthew 6:25

The Lake House

My husband and I decided it was time to look for a new home. Quickly, I found and fell in love with "the Lake House." I loved everything about this house, but the most spectacular quality was the view from the front windows. It was a beautiful large pond, and the way the sun made the water dance was breathtaking. There was only one problem. The day after I found the house, it was taken off the market. This small inconvenience didn't stop me. I called the realtor, and he was kind enough to ask the owner if I could walk through her home in hopes that she would put the house back on the market and we could quickly snatch it up. She agreed, and my obsession was solidified. Walking through the house began a two-year relationship with a home that would never become mine. When I look back now, I do believe that if it were physically possible for a house to get a restraining order, the Lake House would have done so.

Let me explain . . . The owner would change her mind often regarding whether or not she was going to indeed sell her home. We were led to believe that eventually she would do so. That's all I needed. I had a contractor walk through the house with me, and I designed and picked out materials to make the changes I wanted. I even researched who maintained the pool on the property so I could investigate the current shape that the pool was in. This may sound crazy, but that was only the beginning. I began to walk my dogs on the street. That's right. I parked my car at the end of the road and walked my dogs. I met the neighbors. I would demand that my husband took that way home so that he could report any changes in the status of the house. During my lunch break, I drove to the house and ate my lunch by the pond. I would read my Bible, of course, while I claimed the house mine "in Jesus's name." Who does that? I'll tell you who . . . me! Keep in mind that this went on for almost two years. I was beginning to feel that the police passing by my parked car wasn't a coincidence.

As hope dwindled, I began to bargain with the Lord. I also set a fleece. "Lord, if the blue heron is sitting on the rock across the pond when I drive by, I will take that as a sign that I am to wait patiently and not look at any other houses." Pretty sure even God thinks I was overdoing it. As a last-ditch effort, I called the realtor and told him to please convey to the owner that we were going to buy another home. As in, "Listen, I will start seeing other people, I mean properties. Just watch me!"

Fast-forward to the lesson learned and what has happened. The Lord had other plans, greater plans than I could imagine. We did buy another house. The house that I was always supposed to live in with my family. The home I pray I live in forever. I have a very large family; and it is at this house and in this yard that we gather, celebrate, and make memories. We are raising chickens and growing a garden. The house itself is exactly what I wanted, and it makes my heart sing to be able to walk within its walls. I walk grateful that the Lord knows me better than I know myself and that he always has a plan . . . a good plan. When doors close now, I am quickly reminded that I have asked the Lord to be the author of my life, and if he is closing a door (literally in the Lake House case), it is because he is all knowing, all loving, and that the door that he opens will be where I am supposed to be.

By the way, the blue heron . . . he wasn't there.

Proverbs 3:5–6

Jeremiah 29:11

An Apology to My Husband

When our washing machine stopped spinning and draining a month ago, my husband Tom and I gave each other a high five to congratulate ourselves for being so smart. We got this . . . we had bought the extended warranty. Although we were disappointed that the machine was already broken, we were thankful to not have to spend money to replace it.

Fast-forward four weeks. The machine is in pieces in my laundry loom, we have spent hundreds of dollars and valuable time at the laundry mat, and Tom's blood pressure has soared to new heights. We've had to be home on three separate days for an eight-to-five window, and to fix the machine, they literally sent four gigantic boxes of parts to our home. All of this to tell us that the machine could not be fixed and they would contact us regarding how the insurance company would proceed. Also, fun to note that during this month, we have had the stomach bug in our home . . . twice! A working washing machine sure would have come in handy.

Being the strong Christian helpmeet that I am, I have spent a good amount of time talking my husband of the small claims court ledge. Many conversations ended with me encouraging him to "stay in peace" and "shine God's love."

The following is a text that occurred three days ago.

ME. Any news on the washing machine?

TOM. Yes, three more days before we find out how far they are going to stab us! Just found out they will reimburse us up to a whole twenty-five dollars for laundry mat use. Hahaha ugh!

ME. Let's just thank God for our blessings and move forward.

"Move forward." To Tom, this was no longer about spending money to replace a machine we had for two short years; this was about principle.

Yesterday, when the call came in, from the warranty company, I could hear Tom's voice rise. Obviously being of a better sound mind and a closer walk with Jesus, I started to pray, "Holy Spirit, move mountains. Please help Tom to stay patient and kind." I know what you're thinking . . . a little dramatic. But this runaround had been occurring for four weeks. Thank God, I am clothed in strength and dignity, I am so steadfast in my faith, and I was there to lift the situation up to the Lord because a thought occurred to me . . . "It was time for me to take over."

After Tom ended that phone call, I decided to call them back. It took approximately three minutes of their explanation that it would be another five to seven business days for us to receive an answer, regarding how they were going to move forward, that I lost my cool. Stay in peace . . . right! I was crazed. I told the representative that I would be contacting a lawyer and that I wanted to speak to her supervisor immediately. Better yet, I wanted to speak to every supervisor that she had ever worked for. Furthermore, I had zero interest in her spiel that she continued to repeat over and over. I made myself very clear as I screamed into the phone.

I am sure that this poor lady had a drink, with my name on it, that evening. After hanging up, I was instantly humbled and had to apologize to my husband and thank him for not smothering me in my sleep . . . "shine God's light." I did a great job there. We still haven't heard back from the warranty company, but I am confident that I will let Tom take that phone call.

My Life Is His

When I was little, I attended Kid's Church in the basement of our church. One night, for our viewing pleasure, the church showed a movie on the end times. This particular movie was about the journey of two teenage girls after the rapture. They had been "left behind." While left on earth, they became Christians, and when they stood in their faith, instead of denying it, they had their heads cut off by a guillotine. At the end of the movie, the pastor stood in the front and asked if anyone wanted to ask Jesus into their heart. You better believe little Shelley did. She was no fool. If you needed Jesus in your heart to go to heaven, head intact, I was your "yes" girl. I stood on my chair hand raised to the sky and yelled, "Me, me, me!"

I have asked Jesus to be the Lord of my life from a sincerer place than fear (although hell does seem pretty horrifying . . . gnashing of teeth and all), and what a journey it has been. It has been filled with rebellion, church and preaching trends, endless lessons, anger, tears, and joy. It has always been filled with God's grace, forgiveness, and his goodness. Even when I didn't deserve it, which is always.

I have been on fire for Jesus, and when I felt I had it all figured out and could do things in my own strength and wisdom, I walked as a casual Christian. You know, checked in with God here and there. Obedient when convenient and then confused when things became messy. "Where are you, Lord?" This is what I've learned. This never works. Oh, God has been faithful and patient, but I was a ship being tossed by every storm that came my way.

Today, I do not have it all figured out, but I have asked the Lord to help me be the person he created me to be . . . the wife, mother, and warrior for Christ. God created me with gifts and a purpose. I want to live in that plan. He has created you for a wonderful kingdom purpose as well, and your future is one of hope. If you ask God to help you, be the person he created you to be and willing to follow where he leads. Be prepared to have your life and heart transformed in amazing ways. Hear this . . . it is not easy. I have spent a lifetime building up defenses and bad attitudes. Dying to self is a daily challenge. Choosing obedience over feelings can seem impossible. Remaining silent and trusting that God, in all his Sovereignty, is working out the details and fighting my battles, has been one of the more difficult parts of my journey. Forgiving, praying for and serving those that hurt me (really, God?) is no cake walk either. But I have seen too much of God's goodness and his kindness to turn back now. I have seen him make way when there wasn't one. He has saved me.

My life is his.

If you have also seen the movie about the end of times, please contact me. Maybe we can get a group rate for therapy.

John 14:23 says, "Jesus replied, 'Anyone who loves me will obey my teaching. My Father will love them, and we will come to them and make our home with them.'"

Come to Me

S everal years back, my husband wore a T-shirt with the scripture "Come to me, all who are weary and burdened, and I will give you rest" printed on it. I hate to tell you that this T-shirt elicited behavior from me that was unbecoming of a Christian woman, covered in strength and dignity; but it's true. This behavior included eye rolls, snickering, and internal anger. I eventually told my husband that he should no longer wear the T-shirt as it was "false advertising." The worst part is I could not figure out why I hated this T-shirt or more importantly the scripture so darn much. During my soul-searching, this is what I came up with:

    a. Although well intentioned, I'm sure, I have had Christians throw this scripture at me as a Band-Aid during difficult times in my life.

    b. I have felt weary and burdened once or twice or 782 times in my life and not so sure I have felt this rest that the T-shirt and scripture speaks of.

    c. Maybe my husband had figured out this rest, and well . . . I have walked with the Lord longer . . . so what the heck?

Throughout the past few years, I have gained a better under-standing of this scripture. "Come to me . . ." It requires action on my part. I feel the Lord is saying, "Spend time with me. Pause in your much-too-busy life, and be still in my presence. Trust in my promises." "Trust me," "Talk to me about what burdens you, and trust that I am already making all things good for you," "Know my love for you."

What does this look like for me? Finding a quiet space to read his word, putting on worship music that reminds my heart of his comfort, goodness and grace, praying alone, praying with friends, fellowshipping with loved ones and sharing about what God is doing in our lives, and sharing God's love with others.

Just a few weeks back, I was becoming the worst version of myself. I was irritable, angry, and pretty sure that I was not a lot of fun to be around. (Thank God for the amazing people he has placed in my life who love me despite myself.) I thought back on this T-shirt and knew what I had to do. "Come to me . . ." I decided that during the upcoming weekend, I would do just that. I cancelled all plans, made sure I had clean pajamas, and hold on to your hats soccer moms; I arranged rides for my sons to get to their soccer games. It was glorious! I read devotionals. I read his word. I read my favorite Christian authors, and I listened to worship music. I thanked my heavenly Father for all of his blessings. I brought my burdens to him as well. I was in the presence of my Savior. I found his rest and was ready to get back into the race that he has set before me with renewed strength.

Come to think of it . . . . I am kind of wishing I didn't "misplace" that T-shirt.

Matthew 11:28–30
Romans 8:28

Feelings Are a Liar

For the one who sows to his own flesh will from the flesh reap corruption, but the one who sows to the spirit will from the Spirit reap Eternal life.
—*Galatians 5:8*

Feelings are a liar. This is one of the greatest lessons that I am trying to teach my children. We get ourselves in a world of trouble and disappointment because we make decisions based on how we feel. As impossible as it may appear, I want my children to learn to do what is right even when it feels wrong or difficult.

Not even a week into the new school year, Lord, have mercy, my thirteen-year-old son Christopher was faced with this very challenge. On snap-chat (Satan's playground), a classmate had posted what appeared to be a threat to the school they attend. I saw this and reported it to the principal of the school. Because I am an adult. The classmate, let's call him Brian, was questioned the next day and was also informed that it was me that e-mailed the principal. I certainly didn't care. However, Christopher is now the recipient of threats and bullying at school. How do I parent this?

I prayed and went to the Bible. I talked to Chris about Jesus being the strongest man in the world. Jesus did what was right. Always. He has given us example after example of how to do what is right. Jesus had a job to do and did not have time to be offended or live a life controlled by his feelings. I am pretty sure he didn't "feel" like being betrayed, persecuted, beaten, spit on, and nailed to a cross. But he lived a life that honored his Father. He did what was asked of him . . . He did what was right. So we prayed. We asked for wisdom. We prayed for Brian. One morning, we had Chris's friend in the car with us, and when I said, "Let's pray for Brian," Sam responded, "He doesn't deserve it." I explained that it feels that way, but we are instructed to pray for our enemies and those who persecute us (Matthew 5:44).

When I spoke to the assistant principal, I explained what I was hoping would be the outcome of the situation. (1) (best-case scenario) Christopher has the opportunity to befriend Brian. Hurt people hurt other people. There is a brokenness in Brian, and Chris is good people with a heart for his peers. (2) The situation just goes away. We put it in God's hands, leave it there, carry on. (3) Chris is confronted physically, defends himself, and Brian doesn't get hurt. Chris only looks small. Trust me I know violence *is* never the answer. Chris knows Jesus just walked on when confronted. He didn't defend himself. But Chris is a thirteen-year-old boy who spent last year walking away when bullied. I have encouraged Chris to not grow weary of doing good (Galatians 6:9), but I'm not making any promises this time around.

Sigh. I confess that I have gotten to the point that I no longer know how to pray for this. I know God sees every detail, knows every heart and motivation, knows the bigger picture. I have asked for his will alone and will not let it steal my peace or Chris's peace. I will continue to have a lot of conversations with Chris as there are many life lessons that the Bible speaks truth to in this situation: turning a cheek (Matthew 5:38–39), praying for your enemy, trusting God (Isaiah 41:10) to name a few.

Feelings are a liar (Proverbs 3:5). How I desperately want my children to understand this. I may "feel" like smothering my snoring husband, but it doesn't make it right. Seriously, how many problems and destruction come from acting on our feelings? Broken relationships, divorce, missed opportunities, hurt feelings, road rage, yellow cards, murder. I may feel tired, grumpy, irritable, that doesn't make it all right to be unkind to others.

I want my children to know that if they can gain control over their feelings, they can be brave when they feel scared, they can press on when they feel like giving up, they can love when they feel hateful. They can be a leader when they feel like following. They can behave like the son/daughter of God when they feel worthless. They can fight for the less of these when they want to be passive. They can be kind to the bully, maybe even befriend him, when they want to punch him in the face.

I want to live a life that honors God, not for gain but because of what he has done for us. He alone can be trusted. Let's teach our children so that they can shine the light where feelings control us in the darkness.

June

During family altar time at my church, I watched a young woman kneel down. I didn't know her but felt lead to walk down and put my hand on her shoulder and pray for her. As I was praying, I began to cry. The Holy Spirit was up to something. At the end of the prayer, she stood up looked at me and hugged me like a long-lost friend. The pastor began to encourage everyone back to their seats, as she was explaining to me that she felt drawn to me and was hopeful that we could talk. I suggested meeting at the café upstairs after the service. This would give me time to pray that Jesus show up for that conversation as I was clueless as to why she wanted to speak to me.

I began by asking her to tell me about herself. Let's call her June. June is divorced, has four boys (God bless her), and is suffering from anxiety. She has been attending church with her mom off and on for quite some time, and here's the kicker . . . She always looked for me. June went on to say that she watched the way I worshipped and interacted with people, and she felt drawn to me. Was I flattered? Nervous? Let's go with both. (Fellow Christians, the world is watching.)

June shared her heart. She is feeling defeated. Her ex-husband is trying to get full custody on the grounds that she is an unfit mother. June believes that his motivation is financial in nature and that he doesn't want to pay child support. The relationship is toxic and abusive, and she feels zero chance of freedom from him because she is relying on him financially.

I understand this. There was a time in my life that I was tired of feeling that child support was another term for *handout*. I felt oppressed by the fact that my ex-husband was not willingly paying child support; and I decided that if it didn't come out of his heart, wanting to provide for his children, then I didn't want it. There are many amazing moms and dads who do right by their children and support them financially even when divorced. And then there are those who either don't or feel that they can control the other parent because of that money. It becomes oppressive, and I wanted no part of it. People, in my life, would encourage me that it was right for my ex-husband to provide financially for his children but I was not interested in the fight. This was a pretty bold attitude since I was living on a teacher's salary. I believe that God is who he says he is, so I wrote him a letter (something I began when I was a young girl) and asked him to provide a job that would allow me to provide for my children in the absence of support from their father. Within a week, I received a phone call that changed my life. I was being offered a job to work as a behavior analyst to provide support to families with children with autism. The job paid more than my wildest dreams, and I have been working with this amazing organization for seven years. It is one of the best parts of my life and also allows me the freedom to support my children. Praise the Lord!

I told June my testimony, and she responded, "I don't have that luxury." She is referring to the fact that she doesn't think she can ever provide for her children on her own. Neither could I, but God is the Great Provider, and he made a way for me. But she feels less. June feels that maybe God loves me that much, but that it's not the same for her. Somehow her sins are greater. She feels that this is her lot in life. She feels defeated. I know the heart of my heavenly Father, but June has yet to experience this, so she feels hopeless. I ask her if I can pray for her. She says yes. I simply talk to God. I tell him that I know he loves June and sees her pain. I tell him that he alone can make a way. We pray for the heart of her ex-husband and for physical and emotional healing for June. Mostly, we pray for June to experience the love of her Father and that she turns to him as he is faithful and can be trusted. I know God has her in the palm of his hand, and I pray she continues to seek him as he is the answer.

I continue to pray for June and her family and will walk along side of her. God is the master of transforming lives, and I am believing this for her. This is a piece of what the world needs. Christian friends that will stand in the gap. Maybe they haven't accepted Jesus as their Savior; but they need his help, peace, and comfort. We can be the hands and feet of Jesus. We can help and pray for them. We know the Father's love, and we need to share that love when possible and continue to be their hope when they are hopeless.

Generations of Faith

My mother's rock-solid unmovable faith is without a doubt one of the greatest blessings in my life. A blessing that wasn't fully realized until I was a grown woman with my own family. When my mother was twenty-eight years old, she was living in poverty with my dad, who was an alcoholic. At that time, they had four children. Sitting outside, with my baby brother in her arms, she simply whispered to Jesus, "I need you." My mother's walk with Jesus began on that day. Her faith is the kind that petitions the Lord to move mountains for her family . . . and he has. Hours upon hours of prayers to her heavenly Father has made a huge impact on my life and the lives of my siblings. My mother refers to it as the "Jesus Factor," and it is a treasured gift.

Looking back on the difficult years of my childhood, I see a woman who was bold and brave. A woman clothed in strength and dignity. One who responded with kindness and love to the rebellious years of a teenage daughter with a big attitude and big mouth to go with it. I know . . . I shouldn't talk about my sister like that. Kidding. I remember one tantrum in particular where I said such cruel things about this Jesus she loved. I basically told my mother that she was a fool for believing in him and that if he would just show up (in the way, I wanted with all of my infinite wisdom at the age of eighteen), then maybe I would believe as well. You know that whole "If God was a loving God" stuff. She gently and simply replied that she felt badly that I was hurting, but it hurt her for me to say such terrible things about the Jesus, who had saved her and whom she loved. She wouldn't stand for it. Such grace. I tantrum less often these days;

however, I am continually met with that same grace. Grace that has taught me that faith isn't about religion but is about a real relationship with Jesus.

My mother, now a grandmother, has the same commitment to prayer for her grandchildren. What a blessing. She also has served as a foster mother for more than thirty children and has also adopted a young boy. This is an act of love and submission to God. Being a foster mother requires great sacrifice, and it recently seemed that these sacrifices were beginning to take a heavy toll. My siblings and I were concerned. When I asked my mother why she continued to open her home and heart to new foster children, she quickly answered, "Because God asked me to." End of story.

What we do and how we do it matters, especially when it is work done with our heart's intention of serving the Lord. Although the work can be difficult, it does not go unnoticed. I am so grateful for my mother's example to my children. My mother makes it her job to pour the love of Jesus into them. Her life's commitment to children, who need a loving space, has been a positive influence of faith to so many, including her grandchildren. She is a pillar of *faith* and an example of God's love. I often joke that my friends are only friends with me so that they can get to know my mother. I get it . . . She is incredible!

Be Bold

You have all heard of the flight or fight response, right? Much to my husband's dismay, I was created with the fight response. The innocent man, who mistakenly got into the driver's side of my car while I was in the passenger's seat, probably doesn't love this fact about me either. He didn't know what hit him. Good thing my punches don't carry much weight. But that's a different story. The story I want to tell you involves a tragic accident that happened on the road where my son was playing soccer.

While watching Chris on the field, I heard a man screaming, "Help me. Please help me!" I ran to the voice as quickly as I could. It wasn't a choice. When I arrived at the road, I saw a woman lying under a parked car. Quickly, the reality of the situation was revealed as the gentleman yelling started to frantically explain that the woman had fallen off the back of his motorcycle. When I think back on this day, I am still in awe of the Lord's presence. At the field that day, there was a nurse, a physical therapist, bystanders waiting to be called into service, and an amazing woman who would quickly become the injured woman's voice and advocate. There was no time to waste, and those who had the medical background got to work. Stabilizing the woman under the vehicle, she was moved just enough for medical intervention. I do not have a medical background, but I do know the Greatest Physician and knew I needed to intercede for this woman, who appeared to be dying. I took off my available clothing to be used as bandages and knelt at her feet. I put one hand on her and lifted the other hand to the air in petition for her life to be spared.

I asked the only one who could save her.

The ambulance arrived, and the medical team took over. I began to wonder if I was going to be asked to leave. I wasn't. While praying, I heard a woman's voice. She was firmly asking for the life flight to be contacted. Her request quickly became a demand. I think back and wonder if I would ever be bold enough to stand in the gap like that for a stranger . . . to demand that a stranger in need had those needs met. In addition to the accident happening where there were people available with the willingness and knowledge to help, we were also feet away from a field where a helicopter could land. When the men at the field were asked to move nets and equipment to make way for the life flight, there was zero hesitation.

Are there times that you want to help but feel helpless? That day, I wasn't equipped to help. There were other's there that God had equipped for just a time as this. I could pray, though . . . and that is what I did. I asked the Lord for strength to be bold, and I knelt on the road doing the only thing I was equipped to do at that time. There have been many times where I have felt poorly equipped to help. The Lord reminds me that I may not know what to do, but he always knows. So I pray. I want to encourage you to always do what you can to help others, but when you don't know what to do . . . be bold. Remember that your heavenly Father has the answers, and what you may be called to do is to pray. And that is everything.

Hate Hormones

I want to let you in on a little secret . . . I suffer from hate hormones. I have been told, by wiser women than me, that they are genetic. My aunt coined the phrase, and I fear my daughter may suffer as well.

Let me explain. Nothing is different than yesterday. I loved everything and everyone yesterday. Those very same things today . . . I hate. On my way to work this morning, I was listening to a sermon. The pastor said that she challenged herself to spend an entire day either being sweet and positive or remaining silent. I thought, *What a lovely idea. I'm going to do that.* I had no idea I would be suffering from hate hormones exactly twenty-seven minutes later. Jesus help me. What is it? Not enough sleep? My bad diet? The fact that the entire world has gone bonkers? See those things would make sense except that was the story with my life yesterday, and yesterday, I was loving and of sound mind. Today, I want to start a grass roots movement of hatred.

Now don't get me wrong; I am a mature lady of strength and dignity, so when I gave the bird to the person in the car that cut me off, I did it so she couldn't see. It is always on days like this that my son does things like tells me he wants his birthday party tomorrow. Oh, you read that correctly, tomorrow. On a Thursday. He has probably already invited everyone. "No big deal, Mom." Or he has a payment due yesterday, and I have about seventeen cents in the bank.

Am I being tested? That's it, isn't it? I preach a lot about having a positive attitude, and today, I can't run fast away from myself.

There are some positive components to having hate hormones. When I am "suffering," I get crap done. You have a "phone call" you have been putting off? I'm your girl. Neighbor has been letting his dog poop in your yard? Let me at him. You need encouragement? I'm your "let's do this" warrior. My house shines. My mood is better spent scrubbing the floors than telling every member of my family all the reasons I envision poking their eyes out. Leave your wet towel on the floor again . . . do it. Scary thing is I picked that towel up yesterday with a smile and thought, *Oh . . . that kid.* I need therapy, right?

Here are some of the things that I try to snap out of it: pray and say every scripture I know concerning the attitude of my heart and then ask the Lord to supernaturally take over my countenance because I have cussed twice while praying; listen to praise music on the radio and end up yelling things like, "You are still fund-raising?"; taking a hot bath with pretzels and caramel sauce while looking at Instagram and feel numb while scrolling through feeds that usually inspire me (just got out of the tub before I started writing this). Count my blessings . . . I have many, but they don't move me today. Today, I am trying something new. Today, I am writing.

This is helping.

When I think about how God must feel about me on days like this, I am thankful that I know the truth. He loves me, maybe even laughs a little? He knew what he was getting when he invited me into relationship with him. He knows everything about me. He is not surprised by me. God knows that I want to be everything he created me to be, but there are days that I forget to lay it all down or just choose not to. Not my best decision or best days. He always blesses me, though. For example, as I am writing this, an amazing friend told me she posted a song to my time line. I just listened . . . twice. It is perfect. It is God's *grace* and *mercy*. How does he do it? He just loves us so much. I am undeserving and want to just fall into his arms and cry. But I'm too grumpy and stubborn to even do that.

Oh, sweet joy comes in the morning, and I am so thankful. I have work to do that's for sure. My guess if I can pass this test, maybe I will be healed of my hate hormones.

I know I will feel better and hope if you "suffer" as well, you will walk with God on those days knowing that nothing can separate you from his love. If you ever need to be talked off the "I hate everything" ledge, I'm here. I get it.

Hope

"Hope deferred makes the heart sick, but a dream fulfilled is a tree of life" (Proverbs 13:12).

I consider it a blessing and an honor to meet people who allow me to be part of their story and in return become part of mine. I have met many people who suffer with anxiety, depression, and despair. There is a common thread amongst my new friends . . . hopelessness. They have lost hope that they will beat their addictions, get out of their financial hardships, or have their marriages restored. They have lost hope for their own healings or the healings of loved ones.

For many years of my life, I was the president of the "Where are you, God?" school of thought. I also kicked in the "If you even exist" footnotes, with a side of "If you are a loving God, how could . . ." Now when I meet people who live there, I love them instantly. I see their disappointed heart, and I want them to know I understand. Recently, my fourteen-year-old son was injured. He quickly said, "Jesus could have protected me, and he didn't." I hear you, kid. I've been there. I can't be upset with his thinking. I have found joy in watching my children navigate through their relationship with the Lord. Jesus understands their hearts and loves them too much to leave them in their wrong thinking. I trust God with their lives and minds. It wasn't pretty, but everything I have been through has been worth the relationship and trust I have in Jesus. I want to protect my children from making the same mistakes along the way, but sometimes, it is in the mistakes that a real relationship with Christ is born.

It has been quite a journey. I now live in the "God is the only hope" school of thought. I have seen him make a way when there wasn't one. I have seen his goodness. I used to go through a difficult situation doubting God's love for me and, then once through it, look back and say, "Okay, I see what you did there." Many of the times, it was for my own growth. Now when things get messy, I say, "I don't understand what's going on, but I know you do, and I trust you." He always sustains me through the difficult times. God makes a way, heals me, restores me, changes my situation, and changes me. I often feel joy and can't explain why. He is the lifter of my head and allows me to walk in peace as I trust him with my life.

And don't even get me started on Jesus. The more I get to know him, the more I like him. Keep in mind, I've been a "Christian" my whole life. If there has been a sermon, I've heard it. It can get a little chaotic in my mind. My walk has swung from living rogue under grace to legalism under the law. What a mess! Now I want to just know Jesus. I want to know how he lived. I want to know the heart of the Father. I want to walk this life out with them . . . It *is* an awesome adventure.

Because I know the joy of my salvation and the hope in Christ, I want others to know this as well. I love reading his words and experiencing his promises, and I want others to know his transformational power. The more I know him, the more I want to know him. He is my joy . . . my everything. So when I see someone suffering, I want to hug them and tell them, "Jesus sees you." He wants to be your personal Savior and then change you and your life for the best. Everything other than seeking his will for your life, resting in his mercy and grace, and walking out in the truth of his love is temporary and empty. The world needs Jesus. I want to be part of that story.

I want to encourage you to be part of that story as well. Your neighbors feel hopeless. They feel trapped by the things of this world. They need truth, healing . . . God's goodness. You may be just the person that speaks that into their life. Maybe you can be the one who tells them that Jesus came to heal the broken world . . . to heal their broken world. We may not understand why things happen, but we can share our testimonies. We can listen, encourage, and be the hands and feet of Jesus in their lives. We can remind them that they are precious, and we can love them with God's love.

"May the God of hope fill you with all joy and peace as you trust in him, so that you may over flow with hope by the power of the Holy Spirit" (Romans 15:13).

Humble Pie

I hate grocery shopping. Probably has something to do with growing up poor and having times in my adult life that grocery shopping was financially difficult. Anyway, that's a different therapy session. Recently, I was angry with my husband and had the fortunate realization that he had left his bank card in my pocketbook. All of a sudden, grocery shopping seemed like a glorious idea. And I was not going to mess around. I was shopping the outskirts of the store. Ten-dollar organic apples, I'm buying you even though I'm sure you don't taste any different, but I don't care, because I won't eat you. Fresh baked cookies, handmade pasta, fresh soup . . . done. Wait . . . there is a butcher here? All the things that I usually pass by . . . mine. I have been putting off buying new mascara—not today. Thirteen-dollar grocery-store mascara that promises to make my lashes amazing . . . get into my basket. I was practically singing through the aisles.

I walked up to the counter feeling pretty happy with myself. Yes, I was. Then I put Tom's card in and see an emergency message pop up on the screen. It is telling the cashier to "*hold the card.*" Oh no! Apparently, Tom had reported the card lost or stolen. You have to be kidding me! (I am actually reliving the anxiety as I write this.) I now go into explain mode, swearing that I am his wife even though my license says *Rivelli*. Tom's last name is Young. Jesus, help me, I do not want to go to jail . . . or worse have to call my husband. Fortunately, the cashier believes me or feels very badly for me because I am apparently having a nervous breakdown and allows me to put the ridiculous groceries with their ridiculous price tags on my *own* bank card.

Just a little bit of humble pie for my pride. Worst part . . . the mascara is a farce. But who am I to judge?

Letter to My Children

To my dearest Haley, Christopher, and Benjamin,

Because we are not promised tomorrow, and there is so much I want to teach you. I have decided to write it down. I am not sure you have heard me, through your headphones and strong wills, so I am taking the time to put it down in writing. I wish I could wrap what I've learned in a beautiful present for you to unwrap, internalize, and live by; but I am aware this journey is yours. But, alas, I am your mother, so here it goes . . .

Heads up, the following contains lots of capital letters and exclamation points!

If I could only guide you with one instruction, it would be this . . . CHOOSE JESUS! Find out who he is—not who the world says he is but what the Living Word (YES, YOUR BIBLE, you know that book on your shelf) says he is. Talk to him. Have a relationship with him. Spend time with him. EVERY SINGLE DAY.

Friendships. Be the friend you want in return. Love your friends fiercely. Do not tell their secrets. Do not talk about them behind their back. EVER. Always be there to listen, have their back, and encourage their dreams. Be honest. Be their cheerleader in life! Pray for them.

Ownership. Sweet ownership. We all screw up. Own it. Ask for forgiveness often. Set aside your pride always. HEAR ME . . . The only behavior you can control is your own, so don't try to control others. In the same sense, forgive easily. Don't carry resentments that will eat away at you. Let it go! Give it to God. I promise he will take care of it.

Success. Work hard and honest. You have a calling on your life. Think about your gifts and what awakens your compassion. Combine the two. Having arrived is not the following . . . A big house, expensive car, and overpriced clothing and toys. Having arrived is living your life for others. Material things are nice, and I want you to have things that make you smile, but, my sweet children, they are temporary, so be sure to give them their proper place in your hearts and life. If you can learn to do what is right even when it is so hard or feels wrong, you are going to succeed!

His will. This one is superimportant, so pay attention. This one is very difficult, and I understand that. If you can live a life asking God for his will in your life and not your own, HALLELUJAH! What do you know, anyway? He knows whom you should hang out with, which college you should go to, what to study, whom to marry, where to live. He knows *everything*! I promise you that his will and his way is always best! Always! Ask the Lord to help you trust him, because it can be so hard. There will be times that you won't want to ask the Lord to reveal his will about an area in your life. This is because you are pretty sure it may not be what you are hoping for. Trust me, he knows better, and there is a plan. A good one. So ask him, anyway, and then ask for the strength to live according to his will. It will be in God's will that you are the safest and most blessed.

Marriage. Okay, listen. I have good advice here. Don't roll your eyes. Ideally, you marry one time. So choose wisely and with a lot of prayer. After the decision to choose Jesus, the next most important decision of your life is who you marry. This person will become the most important person in your life. The person you walk through this life with, raise children with, grow old with. I know. It's big.

Beautiful Haley, oh, my amazing and free-spirited daughter, you were created for greatness. One of the ways you will be great is by loving your husband well. Serve him, encourage him, and make him laugh. Let him know he is adored. Remind him that he is the only, the strongest, and the most handsome man in your world. Focus on his positives because there are many; you married him, right? During the difficult times, remember why. Remind him why he married you.

Your husband will have challenges all day, be the soft space he has to come home to.

My strong, sensitive, fun, and caring sons. You have a job to do here. You are to love your wife as Jesus loves the church. Find out what that means. Cherish and protect your wife. Make her feel like the only woman in your life (and she better be!). Let her know that your day begins and ends with loving her. Encourage her, remember the details of who she is, and give her your support in becoming the woman God created her to be. Let her blossom in the safety of your love.

To all three, be healthy before you enter a marriage so that you are not bringing someone else's life into your hot mess. If you are sick in any way, get help. There is a ton of help out there, not to mention you have Jesus. No excuses! Learn how to be a healthy communicator. You wouldn't join an accounting firm if you couldn't do math. Do not enter a marriage if you can't communicate. You should probably write that one down. It's good.

Remember to always love and honor your partner, even when you may not like them in that moment.

Live fearlessly (under God's direction of course). When Jesus called Peter out of the boat to walk on water, Peter did. He wanted to be sure that it was Jesus first (smart man), but when he knew, he stepped out of the boat. (Matthew 14:22–33 . . . Look it up). *Be a Peter!* Ask the Lord if the voice you hear is his guiding you, and then fearlessly follow.

Be wise. Attend a church that teaches from the Bible. However, do not let the teachings you receive there replace your personal Bible study. There are many trends in teaching, and some will feed your soul beautifully, but the best teacher is found in the pages of the Good Word. Spread the Gospel like it's your job. Because it is! The world needs to know God's goodness and truth. You were created with power, love, and a sound mind. Don't make choices in life that mess with that. But in case you do, God is always faithful to forgive and set your feet back on solid ground.

Each other. Love each other. Love each other's families. Show up for each other . . . spiritually, physically, emotionally, and financially. Show up for each other. That is all!

Raising your children. Find a tribe of people you love and trust, and raise your children with them.

I love the three of you so much that it takes my breath away. My greatest joy is being your mom. My prayer above prayers for you is that you become the person God created you to be. So do that.

Love,
Mom

Living Water

John 4:25–42

The conversation between a Samaritan woman and Jesus at Jacob's well is one of my favorite Bible stories. I could never quite figure out why. Maybe it was because I could relate to this woman as a rule follower. When Jesus asked her for a drink, she reminded him that he was a Jew and she was Samaritan woman (John 4:9). Jews were not permitted to talk to Samaritans. Not to mention, men weren't allowed to talk to women without their husband, and she was indeed without her husband (we will get to that later). Maybe I love this story because Jesus was not a rule follower and his interactions with this woman intrigued me. He didn't care what others thought . . . He cared about her. He had come for her; his mercy and love were after her.

Unpacking the conversation between Jesus and the woman of Samaria, it became very clear to me . . . I am the woman at the well. Jesus explains to the woman in verse 13 and 14, "Whoever drinks of this water will thirst again, but whoever drinks of the water that I shall give him will never thirst. But the water I shall give him will become in him a fountain of water springing into everlasting life." Of course, this woman wants the water. She would love to never thirst again or walk out to the well to have to have to draw water (John 4:15). She isn't getting it . . . Yeah, I've been there sister. We all come thirsty to a well, and we all satisfy our thirst with temporary and artificial means. Jesus is offering a much greater and permanent water. He is offering to share his life with us.

This is where it gets interesting. Jesus asks the woman to go get her husband. Yikes! The woman answers that she doesn't have a husband. Spoiler alert . . . He knows. Jesus knows everything about her. She has had five husbands and is currently living with a man. This is my favorite part. Jesus doesn't lecture the woman. John 3:17 tells us that "God did not send his Son into the world to condemn the world, but to save the world through him." He is the living water that can save her. He is the living water that has saved me. Jesus doesn't shame her but wants to draw her to himself.

So this is where it gets real for me. How many times have I thirst? How many times have I drunk temporary water? Water that temporarily and artificially filled the void. Jesus knows everything about me and wants me to know his healing power, peace, and joy; and I have rejected him. I have swallowed the wrong water. I am beginning to understand this. It's not easy. When I'm hurt or disappointed, I don't always run to his arms or his word. Thank God, I usually end up there. Usually blubbering about how I'm an idiot. He knows.

When I see someone fighting an addiction (of any kind), living in sin, or making any decisions to drink the wrong water, I remember that we are all the woman at the well, and I understand that maybe I am just a little further along in the story where I see who Jesus is. With Jesus by our side, we are able to live in truth, turn from sin, experience God's grace and healing (daily), and then share the good news. That's what this woman did. After leaving the water jar, no longer needing it (I love that!), she went back to the city and said, "Come, see a man who told me all the things I ever did. Could this be the Christ" (John 4: 29)? She's getting it! Verse 39 tells us that many of the Samaritans of that city believed in him because of the word of the woman who testified.

I want to encourage you toward Jesus. He knows us and knows everything about us, and he loves us too much to allow us to continue drinking the temporary and wrong water. I am so grateful for that truth!

Whatever It Takes

"Whatever it takes, Lord . . . please help Haley be the woman you created her to be." If I had known that my heart's cry for my beautiful nineteen-year-old daughter would have landed her in an emergency room psych ward, I may have kept my thoughts to myself. Watching your children go through dark seasons has to be the most difficult part of parenting. Haley's panic attacks increased in frequency, in the spring of 2016. A tragic death of a dear friend caused Haley to lose her ability to cope, and her panic attacks stole my daughter from her family and friends. She became a shell of herself. Wanting to be stronger than her heartbreak, Haley returned to school in the fall and threw herself into her new apartment, her studies, and playing field hockey. Haley quickly learned that this attempt at pulling herself up by her bootstraps was not the answer. She was broken, and she needed help.

The phone rang shortly after 12:00 on an unexpected sunny Friday afternoon. That phone call. My daughter was on the other end of the phone. I could barely understand her through her sobs, but what I did understand was that I had a short amount of time to get to her apartment thirty minutes away to save my little girl from taking her own life . . . from stopping the pain. My faith challenged . . . I swung from desperation to trusting in the Lord, who is faithful, ever present, and close to the brokenhearted. I couldn't see it right away, but what was happening was God was answering my prayer. Haley needed to be broken into a million pieces to be put back together by her heavenly Father. I did my best to pour Jesus's love and promises into my daughter. I stood on the Word of God and told God that I trusted him with Haley's life. You see, as much as I wanted an immediate supernatural healing, I also didn't want Haley to miss out on any of the lessons or blessings I knew were part of Gods plan. "Whatever it takes, Lord."

Pieces of Gods plan . . . Haley is seeking the Lord. She is learning that life is hard and things of this world will disappoint you but those who trust in the Lord will have hope. Haley is learning that being a Christian is not about showing up for church or about being a good person, but it is a relationship with the Lord. She wants to share her life with a man who also walks in that truth. (My heart can barely hold the sweetness of that . . . *Amen! Amen! Amen!*) She is learning that God never intended us to walk this journey alone and the people you walk alongside of may not be who you expected them to be. Haley is learning that God has created her to speak into people's lives as well. I attended a family meeting at Haley's hospital day program. I was overwhelmed and honored to meet Haley's people. People God has provided for Haley during this season and maybe as lifelong friends. They include a fifty-year-old man with PTSD who desperately wants to be the man his family needs, a young woman who is clinging to the hope that her marriage won't end, a woman who wants friends and a sense of belonging, a man who has attempted to end his pain, a young lady who has dreams but can't imagine they could come true. They want to live. They are you. They are me. They are my daughter.

Proverbs 3:5–6 says, "Trust in the Lord with all your heart and lean not on your own understanding; in all your ways submit to him, and he will make your paths straight." I will never look at this scripture the same way. My prayer is that if you are in a dark season, disappointed, broken, and don't understand what God is doing, that you, too, will hold on to this scripture as the life preserver that I do. He is with you. He has a plan. He loves you. My guess is he is just helping you to be the person he created you to be. Whatever it takes.

A thank-you to my daughter, who is brave enough to let me share her story. She hopes it may encourage someone out there . . . more pieces of God's plan.

Into the Fire

Daniel 3:8–30

Have you ever been faced with a difficult circumstance and you prayed and asked God to deliver you from it? I have. I was recently praying for a dear friend and asking God to deliver her from her current situation. During my time with the Lord, he brought my mind and heart to a story in the book of Daniel. In this story, three men, Shadrach, Meshach, and Abed-Nego are brought before King Nebuchadnezzar for disobeying his order to bow down and worship gold images that he had set up. Because of their refusal to bow down to false gods, the king had ordered them into the fiery furnace. In response, the three men of faith reply, "O Nebuchadnezzar, we have no need to answer you in this matter. If that is the case, our God whom we serve is able to deliver us from the burning fiery furnace, and he will deliver us from your hand, O king. But if not, let it be known to you, oh king, that we do not serve your gods, nor will we worship the gold image which you have set up" (Daniel 3:16–18).

Okay. Wait. "But if not"? What? Even if their God didn't save them from being thrown into a furnace, they were not going to bow down to false gods? They are so sure that their God is faithful and able, and even if he choices to not save them . . . so be it? God knows best? Into the fire we go? Now that faith is a serious life goal.

There are so many lessons to unpack in this story.

1. As followers of Jesus, we should obey God no matter what. (Not easy or my favorite.)

2. We are to have no gods above the one true God. Even if they are flashy or, in my case, rustic.
3. There are times that God may not deliver us from our fiery circumstances, but he promises to join us in the fire. *Amen!* We are not promised a trial free life (hello, fallen world), but we are promised that God will never leave us or forsake us. Joshua 1:9, Matthew 28:20, Revelation 21:3, Psalm 23:4, Zephaniah 3:17, Joshua 1:5.

Looking back on the times that I felt that God could have changed my situation but didn't, I see how I grew in my faith and in my understanding of God's character. I can contribute my growth in the Lord and my walk with him to the times that he didn't change what was happening in my life, no matter how painful, but instead came alongside me. Walking alongside me, sometimes carrying me, always providing peace. I have experienced the joy of the Lord in the most unlikely situations, and I am so thankful for those times. I also stand firmer knowing that when storms will come. I am clothed with strength and dignity, laughing without fear of the future (Proverbs 31:25) because I have experienced the faithfulness of my God. He is and will be my strength, shelter, peace, and believe it or not . . . joy!

4. It is important to stand in our convictions as followers.

When we don't, the world looks upon us as hypocrites. Who can blame them? How can we lead others to Christ if we don't have faith in him ourselves? Because of Shadrach, Meshach, and Abed-Nego's resolve to stand in their convictions and faith in God, they were joined in the fire by an angel of God "and the form of the forth is like the son of God" (Daniel 3:25). Unharmed, they walked away from the flames. Are you getting it? Life is going to bring trials. We may not be delivered (only God sees the big picture here), but God will stand with us, and therefore, we can leave the flames unharmed.

We can even leave not smelling like smoke (Daniel 3:27)! What a testimony! King Nebuchadnezzar was a changed man because of the testimony of these three men, which also changed history for God's

Glory! God had a plan. Daniel 3:28–29 tells us that Nebuchadnezzar spoke, saying, "Blessed be the God of Shadrach, Meshach and Abed-Nego who sent His Angel and delivered His servants who trusted in Him, and they have frustrated the king's word, and yielded their bodies, that they should not serve nor worship any god except their own God! Therefore, I make a decree that any people, nation or language which speaks anything amiss against the God of Shadrach, Meshach, and Abed-Nego shall be cut in pieces, and their houses shall be made an ash heap; because there is no other God who can deliver like this."

What is your testimony that others hear and say, "Could only be God." Keep sharing that testimony.

I am grateful that I have not always been delivered from painful times. At the time, my attitude defiantly said differently, but I'm growing. Do I have the faith of Shadrach, Meshach, and Abed-Nego? Not even close. But the good news is . . . God is not done with me. My friends, he is not done with you either.

Waving the White Flag

"And your children will be taught by the Lord,
and great will be their peace" (Isaiah 54:13).

"For the amount of time I pour Jesus into my children and parent them, I should have better children." The exact words I spoke to my mother earlier this week. I know I can't be alone. We teach them about Jesus, take the time to explain character and integrity, shape their behavior, try to be good models, and communicate our mistakes and correct them when needed (one thousand times a day). I should be celebrating my parenting awesomeness, and, alas, I am not. I am hiding in the bathtub praying for grace and wisdom, pleading with the Lord that the promise of Isaiah 54:13 is truth and comes quickly. Come quickly!

"Cast your burden upon the Lord and He will sustain you" (Psalm 55:22). Currently, my burdens are fourteen and nine years old. My feelings toward them swing like a pendulum, from wanting to ship them off to a Third World country, to gain perspective, to wanting to nominate them for the Nobel Peace Prize, because of their hearts for others. It is quite maddening. I want to hug them, strangle them, swoon over them, and run from them . . . often all at once. I want them to grow up so they can acquire better life perspectives, but I also want to freeze time and capture every waking second with them.

"For I am the Lord your God who takes hold of your right hand and says to you, do not fear; I will help you" (Isaiah 41:13). Parents, let's write this promise on the walls of our hearts. I don't know about you, but I do have fears. I fear that the world will influence my sons more than I do. I fear that they will learn lessons the hard way. I fear that they will turn to temporary things of this world to fill the places that only Jesus can. I fear that they will not become the men they were created to be. I fear that I am not a good enough mom to assure that these things won't happen. The truth . . . I am not. My friends, we can't be. We were never meant to do this hard thing alone, and I, for one, am going to stop trying.

My mother is an amazing woman. She is my role model and often the voice in my head. Raising five children in poverty while married to an alcoholic was not an easy task. It was a daunting task that often brought her to her knees, and it was from that position where the majority of her parenting occurred. The hours she spent in prayer for the five of us was immeasurable. When asked how she raised five children successfully, she always gives glory to the Lord. She lovingly refers to it as the Jesus factor. Well, my children and I need a lot of Jesus factor these days.

I pray for my children. You know, for health, protection, guidance . . . soccer game victories. But now I am all in. I am going to speak life from the word of God over them in prayer. I am going to fight this battle on my knees. Don't get me wrong; I am still going to raise them in Christ, pour Jesus and who he is all over their lives, but I am going to spend more time holding the Lord's hand through it all. I am going to trust that he knew what he was doing when he gave me Christopher and Benjamin. It is the desire of my heart that they become whom God created them to be, so where better to go than to their Creator and his living and powerful word?

I have started to speak scripture in prayer for my children. I have included some of my prayers at the end of this writing. I encourage you, if there is an area in your child's life that he/she is struggling with, find scripture that addresses the struggle and pray God's word over your child.

I am waving my white flag. I am turning to my heavenly Father and asking him to be their Father as well.

Some of my prayers (derived from writings by Bob Hostetler):

1. *Salvation.* "Lord, let salvation spring up within my children, that they may obtain salvation that is in Christ Jesus, with eternal glory" (Isaiah 45:8, 2 Timothy 2:10).

2. *Respect (for self, others, authority).* "Father, grant that my children may show proper respect to everyone, as your Word commands" (1 Peter 2:17).

3. *Courage.* "May my children always be strong and courageous in their character and in their actions" (Deuteronomy 31:6).

4. *Joy.* "May my children be filled with the joy given by the Holy Spirit" (1 Thessalonians 1:6).

5. *Perseverance.* "Lord, teach my children perseverance in all they do, and help them specially to run the race marked out for them" (Hebrews 12:1).

6. *A servant's heart.* "God, please help my children develop servants' hearts, that they may serve wholeheartedly, as if they were serving the Lord, not men" (Ephesians 6:7).

7. *Gratitude.* "Help my children to live lives that are always overflowing with thankfulness and always giving thanks to God the Father for everything, in the name of our Lord Jesus Christ" (Ephesians 5:20; Colossians 2:7).

8. *Peace-loving.* "Father, let my children make every effort to do what leads to peace" (Romans 14:19).

Be Free!

What do you do when you feel loss? You know that desperate, confusing, all-consuming loss. Loss of a loved one, loss of a relationship, a job, your health, or a dream. That loss that you have buried deep within you. That loss that has changed you. That loss that has changed your perspective on life and maybe on who God is. The loss that makes you question if there is a God and if there is, where is he? Where is his love? I have experienced such loss.

You've heard a lot of sayings that talk about being strong. You know the "what doesn't kill you makes your stronger" sayings. Through many trials, I have tried to be strong, to keep my chin up, to work harder, to do better. I have tried to look on the positive side and to count my blessings. I remind myself of other's struggles and that I am blessed in comparison. Here is my secret . . . I am still broken. The loss still controls me. I know God's Word . . . his promises. My brain knows these things. So when I feel lonely, disappointed, scared, hurt, confused, or that I am just failing at life, I can quote a scripture that reminds me of God's promises. I feel better. Temporarily. But I am not set free.

I want to share with you where freedom comes from. Ready? Brokenness. It comes from full surrender to the brokenness and in the only One who can put you back together. It doesn't come from being strong through the storm. It comes from trusting and relying on the One who can be strong for you. I have recently experienced a loss that threw me into a storm of doubting, questioning God's love and plan for my life and frankly my own sanity. You know the loss that has you paralyzed on the bathroom floor (to be completely transparent). As much as I reassured myself through scripture that nothing can separate me from the everlasting love of my Father (Romans 8:38–39) and that his plans for me are to prosper me and not harm me and to give me hope and a future (Jeremiah 29:11), it was just a Band-Aid. I don't believe God wants me to use his promises to Band-Aid my hurt. Don't get me wrong. His promises are truth. They are life. But God wants to heal the root of my pain. That loss I have buried deep within. He wants this for you as well! There is a reason we don't make true progress, why we don't find freedom. Why we always end up back in the same place of hurt. We apply God's promises and truth to the surface of the wound and refuse to let him heal the wound itself. It is just too difficult. It hurts too much. We just want to feel good with a fresh Band-Aid. We wash the wound a little, apply some ointment, put a Band-Aid on it, and carry on. Right? Fortunately, God loves us more than that. He wants more for us. He sent Jesus to set us free. Truly free!

In my brokenness, I have to confess to God that I am clueless how to take another step. I feel confused and so hurt. I have to confess that I have tried to be whole by depending on my own thinking, strength, and perspective. I have to let go. This is the hardest part. *Letting go!* I have to allow his supernatural presence and strength to carry me and to heal me. I have to allow him to speak to my wounds and to reveal where his healing power needs to be. It's a battle of wills, my friends. If I surrender and let go what if things don't go the way I want? I know the truth. God's ways and his plans are best, but can I really trust him? Before I only knew with my mind that the answer was yes but now, through my brokenness, I know in my heart the same truth. The answer is yes. He alone can be trusted. He alone is the lifter of my head, my great physician, my rock and fortress. The Lord alone is my provider, my comforter, my Abba Father. My dear friends, confess to the Lord your brokenness, your doubts, confusion, anger, disappointment, and fears. Invite him to reveal to you the root of your wounds, and then to heal your wounds as if they never existed. Invite the Lord to restore the joy of your salvation as a replacement of your wounds, not just a Band-Aid. Be freed in your brokenness. Be free!

John 8:36

One for the Girls

"For the Lord your God is with you. He is a mighty savior. He will take delight in you with gladness. With his love, he will calm all of your fears. He will rejoice over you with joyful songs" (Zephaniah 3:17).

Oh, sweet lover of my soul. How did I take one step before I really knew you . . . before I knew your love for me?

Ladies, how do you define yourself? In Romans 1:25, Paul tells us, "They traded truth about God for a lie." What lies are you believing today? Life can do a number on us, and we begin to see ourselves through the darkness instead of the light. Maybe you were abused or are currently in an abusive relationship and believe the lie that you are unworthy of being cherished. Maybe he had an affair, and you believe the lie that you aren't enough or if you were only prettier, smarter, funnier. Maybe you can't figure out why you can't make or keep friends, and you believe there is something wrong with you. Maybe you feel that the abortion you had or the drugs and alcohol you are addicted to disqualifies you for Christ's love. That's a lie.

But here is the truth. You are Jesus's most prized possession (James 1:18). He invites you into relationship just the way you are. That's right . . . invites you with all that sin, mistakes, and bad attitude. He won't leave you alone. He won't forsake you. And he loves you so much that he won't leave you in your sin. He will change your heart, and you will love him so much you will leave your sin behind. He loves you too much to watch you stay in the muck and mire. He will lovingly correct you. Unless you are stubborn like me, then he will take you behind the woodshed. Either way, it is because of his love for you that he will work out the kinks in your walk with him. He will help you leave the lies behind and give you a new name.

When you fall, he will be cheering for you, whispering in your ear, "I'm here. Get up!" When you are hating on yourself, he will remind you, "Stop believing the lies. You are a daughter of the King!" When you are sad, he will wipe your tears and wrap you in his arms. He will strengthen you and encourage you. When you try things on your own, he will wait patiently and open his arms when you come running back . . . He will whisper, "It's okay. I love you." And if you go missing, he will leave everything to come find you.

Those times you felt rejected, that was just Jesus saying, "Sorry, you're not dating or marrying my girl." Didn't get that job? God has better plans. Rejection is Jesus's fierce protection. My sweet sister, I pray that you don't take one more step without knowing the lover of your soul. Man will disappoint you; Jesus will not. Give him your heart; he can be trusted. I know you have been hurt. Let Jesus rescue you, heal you, and place your feet on solid ground.

The Greatest Commandment

Isn't it fun to get to know new people? I love finding out what their favorites are . . . music, food, movies, season? Do they work out? Do they binge watch any TV shows? How often do they eat pizza? Where do they love to vacation? What do we have in common? What are our differences? What have we experienced that can encourage each other?

When I want to feel close to Jesus, I pretend that I am sitting with him, and I ask him things like, "What's your favorite color? What music do you listen to? What's your favorite food?" I want to know him more. Recently, I have been asking him about what his thoughts are on the current political changes. I have sought council from much smarter Christians than me, I have looked to scripture, I have read countless articles, and I have watched the news. I don't have answers, and at times, I feel ignorant and hopeless. Then Jesus reminds me . . . it's not always my job to know. That's his gig. It is impossible to see the big picture and to know how things happening now fit into the future.

What I do know is this . . . Jesus has a lot to say about loving one another: 1 John 4:7–8, John 13:34–35, 1 Peter 4:8, 1 John 3:16, Colossians 3:12–15, 1 Corinthians 16:14, Hebrews 13:1–5, 1 Thessalonians 3:12, Luke 6:27–36, John 15:12, just to cite a few. There are so many more. However, consider what Jesus says in Mark 12:30–31: "Love the Lord your God with all of your heart and with all of your soul and with all of your mind and with all of your strength. The second is this: Love your neighbor as yourself. There is no greater commandment than these." *No greater commandment than these?* Got it. So when I feel hopeless, I remember that I am not instructed to understand the entire goings on in the world. I am instructed to love and not judge (Matthew 7:1–5). Love. I can work on that. I can start each day asking the Lord to show me how I can shine his love and then be obedient to his direction. I can research ministries that are leading the charges on loving and empowering the poor, the hurting, and come alongside them. I can share the life transforming, chain breaking truth of the Gospel. I can be mindful of the *greatest commandment.*

Don't let the chaos of the world stop you from fulfilling the greatest commandment. Embrace it. Run full speed in it. This is how things will change. How are you going to love today?

In case you are wondering . . . pretty sure the answers are . . . purple, the Brothers McClurg, and pizza!

Forgiveness

Oh, Forgiveness. Sweet, merciful, freeing, I just don't want to do it . . . Forgiveness. Why can forgiving others be so difficult? This is what I have learned:

1. Forgiveness is required even when the other person is not sorry nor has asked for forgiveness. Not my favorite lesson.
2. Refusing to forgive with the hopes that your anger will change the other person's behavior (i.e., "How are they going to feel the consequences of their behavior and see how badly they have hurt me if I forgive them?") never works and telling yourself it does is a lie that chains you to pride and resentment.
3. Jesus is not asking us to do anything that he did not set the perfect example of. Jesus died on the cross for our sins. He was and is the greatest intercessor with the Father to forgive us. It is out of his amazing and unending love for us that he requires us to forgive. He knows that holding onto anger is like swallowing battery acid and will surely lead to death. Forgiving others and allowing him to take over from there leads to peace and freedom. When we forgive others, and at times, we need God's help to do so, we are trusting that God's ways are better than our own.

The Bible has some things to say on this topic. "And whenever you stand praying, forgive, if you have anything against anyone, so that your Father also who is in heaven may forgive you your trespasses" (Mark 11:25). "Be kind to one another, tenderhearted, forgiving one another, as God in Christ forgave you" (Ephesians 4:32). "But if you do not forgive others their trespasses, neither will your Father forgive your trespasses." Yikes! I am pretty sure these aren't just suggestions, and I am a sinner who needs my heavenly Father's forgiveness.

Scriptures that instruct us in forgiveness include but are not limited to 1 John 1:9, Matthew 18:21–22, Matthew 6:14–15, James 5:16, Luke 6:37, Colossians 3:13, Psalm 103:10–14, 1 John 1:9–10, Luke 7:44–50, Matthew 6:12 (part of the Lord's prayer), and Romans 12:17. So clearly not knowing what Jesus has to say about forgiveness is not an excuse. This is not a topic Christians can refer to as a "gray area." It is clear. Forgive.

Growing up with my father was challenging at best. There were many times forgiveness was needed, and that is what I did. Until the time I didn't. My father had been at the bar and was saying unkind things about me. When this got back to me, I decided that I had had enough. It was very important to my father that he heard from his children on his birthday. Well, I was going to show him by ignoring his birthday that year. He let everyone know that I hadn't wished him a happy birthday, and I felt like I had made my point. Well done, Shelley. My brother Doug spoke to me about the importance of forgiving my father, along with the reasons I needed to, and I wouldn't hear of it. Looking back, I know that God sent my brother to talk to me, but I was so blinded by my anger and pride. God always knows best. *Always.* You see, that is why he asks us to forgive and release the hurt and the one who hurt us into his capable hands. God is all knowing. He knows the very details that we couldn't possibly know. He knows the motivations of our heart and of the heart of the one that hurt us. God knows our brokenness, but, dear friend, he also knows the brokenness of the one who hurts us. Please understand, I am not suggesting that you allow yourself to stay in a relationship with someone who is mistreating you. Setting boundaries is important. I am encouraging you to release that person into God's hands and, by forgiving that person, allowing the healing you need to begin.

I never did get to work things out with my father. Days after my brother came to speak to me about forgiveness, my father died unexpectedly in his sleep. When I walked into his living room and saw him on the couch, no longer with us, I threw myself on him and begged him for forgiveness. It was the rawest emotion I have ever felt. It was too late. If I had been obedient to God's Word my father's departure would have been as difficult but not filled with regret. God asks things of us and instructs us in the way to go because he loves us. We are not intended to live chained to anger. Jesus came to set us free.

There is freedom in forgiveness. Chains are broken, and peace replaces anger. God is faithful to take it from there. I am always growing, and I am so thankful for God's patience with me. Forgiveness is freedom and requires a trust in my heavenly Father that he will be right by my side as I release the hurt and the one who hurt me . . . trusting that he will make all things good (Romans 8:28). Be free, dear friends. Let it go. Walk in Peace. God's got this.

Grace

He sat in the back, weeping . . . his Savior's arms around him. The church was so quiet, yet no one heard him cry.

My father was born and lived in the same town for his entire life. He was known by many and loved by most. This truth has always confused me. The only reasoning that makes sense is that my father had a calling on his life; however, he did not live a life worthy of that calling. Grace . . . the free and unmerited favor of God, as manifested in the salvation of sinners and the bestowal of blessings. I have experienced *grace* time and time again in my life. But I have gained a better understanding of grace through the life and death of my father. I had expectations of who my father was supposed to be in my life and later in the lives of my children. I was chained to disappointment because of these expectations. Mercifully, I was eventually released from those chains. God lovingly spoke to my heart about allowing him to be the father I desperately needed and then about releasing my dad from being the father he was not. My only regret is that I did not have more time with this new perspective. Maybe I could have been a listener and encourager in my father's life rather than his judge and jury.

I arose so early on this Christmas Eve (it is still very dark out) because someone needs to hear this message. We are all broken. Some of us are fortunate that we have not become addicts with the attempt to fill in the pieces of our brokenness with drugs and alcohol. My Christmas prayer for you today is that if you are an addict or turning to drugs and alcohol to take away the hurt that you will instead allow God's love and grace to consume you, heal you, and give you a new life. If you are someone who is disappointed with a loved one, I pray that you will pray for them, release them to the Lord, and ask God for opportunities to speak into their brokenness. Be part of their healing story. We all need grace. Every day. It is the very reason we were sent a Savior.

In a few hours, I will go to my dad's grave to sing carols with my family. I have two brothers and two sisters, and we will bring our individual families to sing. It is such a treasured time for me. For me, it is about being with my siblings to honor my father.

Remember, when we trust Jesus to be our everything, we are freed to live a life without expectations of others. When we allow the Lord to meet all of our needs, we can love and encourage others for who they are and not what we need or want them to be in our lives.

Ephesians 2:8–9

Romans 6:14

Act 15:11

Isaiah 9:6

Shine On!

I have an odd fascination with outdoor light fixtures, often taking my eyes off the road to look at them on the houses as I drive by. Maybe it is that there are so many styles, colors, and sizes. Some securely fastened while others hang on by a thread. The Lord brought this thought to me while driving the other day "just like people." And then my Spirit continued . . . all of these light fixtures are different. Some are old and rustic, others new and polished. However, most of them have weathered some kind of storm, perhaps several storms, and yet they are still capable of doing one thing. Shining light.

Dear friend, whether you feel weathered by the storm or are fortunate to feel new and polished . . . shine God's light. If you are weathered by a storm (maybe the storm is raging in your life now) shining light may be by telling your story. Satan would love for you to hide that story, to feel shame about the storm. I want to encourage you that by telling your story, you are shining light. Light into the darkness of someone else's storm. The storm that tells them that they are alone, the only one going through this. The storm that tells them that it is their fault and they deserve the winds and upheaval, that they are unworthy or that what they are living through disqualifies them for God's love. That my friend is the greatest lie of all! *Nothing* can separate you from the love of God! You are his beloved. You are worthy! You are loved beyond measure. You are clothed in *strength* and *dignity*.

As I watch my daughter in her storm of depression, I encourage her to tell her story, to tell of her faith. I encourage her to give thanks in the storm and shine that into other people's stories. Satan knows if you stop shining into other's lives . . . if you stop pouring truth, encouragement, and compassion on others, then you will become the Dead Sea. My friend, that is exactly where he wants you, but he will not win if you shine on! So shine on! Tell your story. Listen to other's stories without judgment but with open hearts and kind words. Ask the Lord to show you where you can help and then move. Run toward people's pain and shine into their storm. I believe in you . . .

John 1:5
Psalm 27:1

A Credit Card and the Love of Jesus

"Suppose one of you has a hundred sheep and loses one of them. Doesn't he leave the ninety-nine in the open country and go after the lost sheep until he finds it" (Luke 15:4)?

Monday. August 21, 2017, 7:27 p.m. A dear friend, Marybeth, posted a need for help ASAP. A homeless woman had been dropped off at a local church. She was in need of shelter that night.

It was 7:32. I replied, "Working on this right now." No clue how I was going to "work on this," but I know my God and that I have a church who walks the walk. I called my pastor's wife and told her what was happening. Within five minutes, we had a room secured at a local motel, and I was on my way to the church to meet the woman in need.

Victoria. Victoria was sitting at the table. God would have it that there was a meeting happening at the time Victoria was dropped off at the church. At that meeting, there was a man I have admired for most of my life. His name is Ray, and he is a blessing to all people. Ray and I brought Victoria to the motel. The conversation flowed easily, and I liked her instantly. Before checking in, the three of us prayed, and I felt sad leaving her there. It is important to note that the motel had four nights available, and no amount of begging or bribing (I tried) was going to change this fact.

Tuesday. August 22, 2017. I spoke to Victoria on the phone several times . . . from the Footbridge Beach in Ogunquit, Maine. Ray was on the job, making calls and exhausting all resources. By the end of the day, every door had been closed. Shelters were turning people away or only taking adults with children. Both Ray and I knew that a shelter was not the answer, but she was looking at living on the streets again in three days.

Wednesday. August 23, 2017. More phone calls pleading Victoria's case. No progress. Ray made an appointment with Catholic Charities. Local counseling resources were also called. Victoria and I spoke throughout the day.

Thursday Morning. August 24, 2017. I picked Victoria up early to spend the morning at my house. I wanted to get to know her better. I wanted to know how I could help. We laughed (belly laughed). We cried. We shared stories and talked about our children. I was once again reminded that we are all one step away from being in Victoria's shoes.

Ten thirty. Meeting at Catholic Charities. Although this organization is amazing, it was not what Victoria needed. We left with a list of other resources and people to call. Back in the car, I felt the Lord prompt me to ask Victoria what she wanted. I could tell by her body language that it had been a very long time since anyone had asked her that. After a long pause, she responded "to be back with my mom and help her and to have relationships with my children." We talked about God being an expert in restoration, and then she added, "And McDonald's." Kindred spirits.

After stuffing our faces with double cheeseburgers nuggets and milkshakes, I brought Victoria back to the motel. I worked the phones, alongside of Ray, and turned up empty. My daughter suggested Teen Challenge in Providence. Brilliant. What could be better? Teen challenge is a faith-based program. My church, as well as my family, has supported this program for years. I called them and was hopeful this was the answer. I secured an intake appointment for the next morning, when I would be with Victoria again. Perfect timing as Victoria had to be out of the motel by eleven the next morning.

Friday. August 25, 2017. Eleven o'clock. Victoria interviewed with Teen Challenge and was told she needed to detox prior to entering the program. She asked me to drive her to a hospital in Woonsocket, Rhode Island. After she was admitted, I asked to speak to the social worker. I was informed that there wasn't one. I broke. Just starting weeping. What do you mean? Taking pity on me, they sent a nurse to talk to me. I gave her all of the contact info at Teen Challenge and reviewed the plan with her. I cried the entire way home. I am still not entirely sure why.

Today, at 7:45 a.m. Victoria called me and informed me that she was being discharged. Not wanting to upset her, I didn't challenge her. I drive to the hospital, pretty sure that she has misunderstood. I'm wrong. It's true. Victoria has been "medically cleared," and because she has MassHealth Insurance, they cannot treat her for a detox. However, they did give us a very handy discharge sheet on the symptoms of alcoholism. Seriously? I couldn't even make eye contact with Victoria. As we turned to walk away, the nurse yelled out, "You're a saint." I knew instantly what she meant and was offended for my newest friend. Victoria is not a burden or someone who I should be thanked for walking alongside. She is my sister in Christ.

At this point, one would think I would be panicked. I wasn't, and let me tell you why. *God knows all.* He knew I was in over my head, so he sent me Melissa. Melissa knew the situation and knew she had the information and grit to help. Victoria and I were headed to her house. To summarize the remainder of the day, thanks to Melissa and to God for sending her, we got an intake at a crisis counseling center. Victoria, who is very medically sick, is at a Massachusetts Hospital while others are working to put a long-term plan in place for her. Melissa was handpicked for this assignment because without her perseverance and knowledge, we would have walked out of the crisis center today with a printed out copy of detox centers to look into. Instead, Melissa may have saved Victoria's life. She confidently laid out the plan, and they got on board.

As we speak, Victoria is at the hospital detoxing. I wonder how she is feeling and will call her soon. Maybe I will bring her some McDonald's.

Thank you, Marybeth, for stepping out in faith for Victoria. Thank you to all the warriors who have been faithful to pray. Please continue to pray. This is Victoria's journey that she can quit at any time. I pray she doesn't. Thank you, Lord, for going after the one.

Thank you, God, for continuing to pursue her. Thank you, Ray, for tirelessly advocating for Victoria and for so many others. Also, thank you for talking me off the ledge, especially when I was outraged by the lack of knowledge and help available. Thank you, Mom and friends, for worrying about my heart. Thank you, Haley, (my daughter), for checking on me to assure that I wasn't over my head. I was . . . all week long.

Friends, please remember that when you are feeling unequipped, God will still call you into action. Go. Hold his hand and run into someone's story. God will provide everything you need. I felt the hosts of heaven this entire week. I told Melissa and I will tell you . . . I have the love of Jesus and a credit card. My skills end there.

Additional Notes

1. Spread the Gospel. Although timing is important. Victoria was curled up in my passenger seat, pale, nauseous, and clueless to where she was going to sleep that night. I turned to her and asked her, "Have you asked Jesus into your heart?" I am laughing as I write this. It's an important question, but pretty sure, she would have gotten out to walk if she could have.

2. For anyone questioning where I rate on the saint scale. During the meeting at the crisis center, I was texting Tom and asking him to make me an appointment for a massage and to make plans to take me to dinner . . . I am not suffering.

The Battle

John 10:10. The thief comes only to steal and kill and destroy; I have come that they may have life, and have it to the full.

How is that going for you? Are you taking hurtful things said about you and to you as truth, or are you seeing them as the lies, spewed from the pit of hell, that they truly are?

This is what Satan does. He doesn't have to be creative. He knows how precious you are; and he comes to steal that away, kill your confidence in Christ, and destroy the very person you were created to be.

Satan doesn't wait until you are an adult. This destruction often begins when you are a child. Satan uses the very people who are supposed to edify and protect you to destroy you. It can be a careless comment made out of frustration by a loved one. Unfortunately, that same person can say a million words of love and encouragement, but the words spoken that were hurtful are placed in the file of truth in your heart and mind. Those very words are the repeat button that has been pressed over and over. I am convinced that the only way to shut those words up are by allowing Jesus to literally come and shut that button off.

I have needed that healing. I know the authority I have, in Christ, to rebuke the lies of Satan. I know that God has loved me and cherished me from the beginning of time. I am his daughter. Yet there are still words that haunt me. I will not rest until I am truly set free, but the fight to believe that I am who God says I am is a battle.

Ten years ago, I was told that "I was useless"—that "I always had been." The person who spoke this to me was an addict and not of sound mind. Do you think that mattered? Not at all. I was crushed. If I allow them to, the words can still rattle me. Why do we allow this? Why is it somehow easier to believe that the lies are truth?

When we allow the lies to be the fabric of our thinking, we miss out on being who God created us to be. We no longer have the confidence in Christ to step out and live a life in victory and to help others do the same. Satan's plan all along.

If Satan can steal the very essence of who you are in Christ, then he can put you on a path of destruction. He takes you and carves out the truth, and then you begin to fill that space with anyone and any- thing that temporally makes you feel whole again . . . or, in the least, temporarily shuts the button off. I have filled this space with wrong thinking, bad relationships, self-pity, and poor decisions. What are you filling your space with? What or who are you putting your hope in to shut that voice of lies up? More of Satan's plan. Do you see it? Satan knows the only answer is Christ. *He knows.* So he is going to work very hard at making sure you don't know.

Freedom. The closer I get to Jesus, the more I hear his voice of truth over the lies of Satan. Nothing else works. Jesus came so that we may have life and have it to the full. That's the life I want. Get out there. Find a church that teaches from God's word. Join Bible studies. Read your Bible. Talk to other believers. Don't let Satan win. He's a liar.

Ephesians 6: 10–17 tells us,

> Finally, be strengthened in the Lord and in the strength of his power. Put on the full armor of God, so that you may be able to stand against the devil's schemes. For our struggle is not against flesh and blood, but against the rulers, against the authorities, against the spiritual forces of evil in the heavenly realms. Therefore, put on the full armor of God, so that when the day of evil comes, you may be able to stand your ground, and after you have done everything, to stand. Stand firm then, with the belt of truth buckled around your

waist, with the breastplate of righteousness in place, and with your feet fitted with the readiness that comes from the gospel of peace. In addition to all of this, take up the shield of faith, with which you can extinguish all the flaming arrows of the evil one. Take up the helmet of salvation and the sword of the spirit, which is the word of God.

Would God give us instructions for battle if there wasn't one? The closer you walk with Jesus and the more you are equipped with God's word, the better prepared you are to dress for battle. To stand against the lies of the devil. To live a full life in Christ. Let's do this, and then let's teach others. I want to be part of the story of leading others to truth and watching them be set free from the lies and the life of destruction. What lies are you believing? What lies are stealing your life from you? Are you ready to be set free?

Warrior Boots

For if you remain silent at this time, relief and deliverance for the Jews will arise from another place, but you and your father's family will perish. And who knows whether you have not come to the kingdom for such a time as this (Esther 4:14)?

As Christians, we walk through many seasons. Maybe you are being called into a season of rest and restoration. What a sweet season, where Jesus calls you into his presence to be healed and refreshed. Lovely Psalm 23:2, "He lets me rest in green meadows; he leads me beside peaceful streams." Maybe you have broken places that need to be healed in Jesus's loving arms. Do that. Rest. Be still.

Maybe you are in a season of confession, repentance, and getting right with the Lord. Acts 3:19 instructs us, "Repent, then, and turn to God, so that your sins may be wiped out, that the times of refreshing may come from the Lord." Be encouraged. Correction comes from the love of your heavenly Father. He loves you far too much to let you stay in sin. Sin leads to death . . . every time. Death of relationships, death to your sound mind and health, death of peace and freedom. Mind you, this is not a fun season. Honestly confessing and turning away from your sin is difficult but necessary. You were created for greater things to waste your life living in sin and ungodliness. You were called to be set apart for the glory of God. I have walked in this season. Being held to the fire feels torturous, but in the end, you walk closer with Jesus in freedom. Closer to who you are created to be. We are called to be mothers, fathers, husbands and wives, brothers, sisters, leaders, workers, friends, and role models. These are important roles. If you are walking in sin, you are not going to honor the Lord in these areas in your life. This season requires you to ask the Holy spirit to search your heart (Psalm 139:23–24).

Maybe you are in a season that requires putting on your warrior boots. This is the season the Lord has called me into. Then I heard the voice of the Lord saying, "Whom shall I send as a messenger to this people? Who will go for us?' I said, "Here I am. Send me" (Isaiah 6:8). So, my friends, I am in the season of the battle. I have replied to the Lord, "Send me." My weapons . . . the armor of God.

If you are in this season and feel that the battle is against another person. It is not. It never was. "For we are not fighting against flesh-and-blood enemies, but against evil rulers and authorities of the unseen world, against mighty powers in this dark world, and against evil spirits in the heavenly places" (Ephesians 6:12). Fighting this battle means praying for those who hurt you. It's about dying to yourself and feelings and being obedient to what the Lord has called you to do. We are not going to hate anyone into the kingdom. Did you hear that? We are *not* going to hate anyone into the kingdom. God calls us to forgive and pray for our enemies. *Not* easy or my favorite. Hence the battle. When Jesus commands us to love the Lord God with all of our heart, souls, and strength, and to love our neighbors as ourselves, he is not making a suggestion or referring to only the neighbors who are our friends. This dying world needs a Savior, and you know him. Who are you sharing him with?

So this is the battle . . . to fight against the lies of Satan. The battle may begin within ourselves. The tools to win that battle are the truths of God's Word. Spend time searching what the Bible says about who you are in Christ and his everlasting love for you. Ask the Holy Spirit to seal those truths in your heart. Let the truth of who you are in Christ replace every lie that Satan has spoken to you. Then spread those truths like it's your job. Because it is. Spread the Gospel and what Jesus did at the cross to this dying and deceived world. They need to know what Jesus told the woman at the well; they need to know that he is the Great I Am. Saturate yourself in his word and then ask him for opportunities to share his chain-breaking, life-transforming truth with others.

Be prepared. Satan does not like to be exposed. He will try and come against you. He always does. Satan knows that Jesus alone is the answer, so when you tighten your warrior boots, he will be watching. *Don't be afraid.* You know the truth; you have been in training. You know what 1 John 4:4 says, "You, dear children, are from God and have overcome them, because the one who is in you is greater than the one who is in the world." Amen!

Some battle tactics. Pray. Battles are won on our knees. Seek wisdom. Share the Gospel. "The Spirit of the Lord is upon me, for he has anointed me to bring Good News to the poor. He has sent me to proclaim that captives will be released, that the blind will see, that the oppressed will be set free" (Luke 4:18).

Give testimony to what the Lord has done in your life. Share your story. "Oh, give thanks to the Lord, for he is good, for his steadfast love endures forever! Let the redeemed of the Lord say so, whom he has redeemed from trouble" (Psalm 107:1–2). Ask the Lord to be used to further his kingdom. To spread the good news. Ask for opportunities to share your testimony for his glory.

Every season is preparation for the next. If you are in the battle, put on your armor of God (Ephesians 6:10–18), grab onto Jesus's hand, and march on. The God of angel armies is with you.

"Have I not commanded you? Be strong and courageous. Do not be afraid; do not be discouraged, for the Lord your God will be with you wherever you go" (Joshua 1:9).

Head up, Soldier! Tighten your boots. It is time.

One More Thing . . .

Becoming who you were created to be begins with letting go. Let go of the sins. First, you have to take ownership of them. "Lord, I confess . . ." Begin there. I know how difficult this is. Trust me. But it's worth it. Put Satan in his place. He's having a field day beating you up about your past. Take ownership, "Yes, I did that, Lord," and ask for forgiveness. Jesus knows the whole story. He knows everything that led up to the sin in your life. He already knows what you need to talk to him about. Let him wash you whiter than snow. Then Satan can take a hike when he comes around to condemn you. The Lord has taken away your punishment and made things new for you.

"Come now, let us settle the matter," says the Lord. "Though your sins are like scarlet, they shall be white as snow; though they are red as crimson, they shall be like wool" (Isaiah 1:18).

I love this! The Lord is saying . . . "Come on, child, let's settle this. Confess your sins. Hand them over . . . l will wash you clean." Hallelujah! Makes me want to dance.

Sweet Psalm 51:7 reads, "Purge me with hyssop, and I shall be clean, wash me, and I shall be whiter than snow." Whiter than snow. Anyone need that right about now?

Enjoy your freedom. There is joy with Jesus. There is laughter. Remember who you are. Remember that you are clothed in strength and dignity. I will be praying for you.

About the Author

S helley Rivelli is a writer, speaker, and a special education teacher. She is a mom to three, wife of Tom Young, and a resident of her home town Northbridge, Massachusetts. Shelley loves her community and is walking this life out, with the Lord, to inspire others to live their best life loved by Jesus.